The Fragmented Female Body
and Identity

MODERN
AMERICAN
LITERATURE
New Approaches

Yoshinobu Hakutani
General Editor

Vol. 56

PETER LANG
New York • Washington, D.C./Baltimore • Bern
Frankfurt • Berlin • Brussels • Vienna • Oxford

Pamela B. June

The Fragmented Female Body and Identity

The Postmodern, Feminist, and Multiethnic Writings of Toni Morrison, Theresa Hak Kyung Cha, Phyllis Alesia Perry, Gayl Jones, Emma Pérez, Paula Gunn Allen, and Kathy Acker

PETER LANG
New York • Washington, D.C./Baltimore • Bern
Frankfurt • Berlin • Brussels • Vienna • Oxford

Library of Congress Cataloging-in-Publication Data

June, Pamela B.
The fragmented female body and identity: the postmodern, feminist, and multiethnic
writings of Toni Morrison, Theresa Hak Kyung Cha, Phyllis Alesia Perry, Gayl Jones,
Emma Pérez, Paula Gunn Allen, and Kathy Acker / Pamela B. June.
p. cm. — (Modern American literature; v. 56)
Includes bibliographical references and index.
1. American fiction—Women authors—History and criticism. 2. American fiction—
Minority authors—History and criticism. 3. American fiction—20th century—
History and criticism. 4. Women in literature. 5. Feminism in literature.
6. Female friendship in literature. 7. Ethnicity in literature.
8. Self in literature. I. Title.
PS374.W6J86   813'.54093522—dc22   2010014260
ISBN 978-1-4331-1050-4
ISSN 1078-0521

Bibliographic information published by **Die Deutsche Nationalbibliothek**.
Die Deutsche Nationalbibliothek lists this publication in the "Deutsche
Nationalbibliografie"; detailed bibliographic data is available
on the Internet at http://dnb.d-nb.de/.

© 2010 Peter Lang Publishing, Inc., New York
29 Broadway, 18th floor, New York, NY 10006
www.peterlang.com

Printed in Germany

For my mother

❋ TABLE OF CONTENTS

Acknowledgments ix

1   Introduction: Multiethnic Fragmentation
      and Women's Community.. 1

2   The Fragmented Body and Maternal Healing:
      The Examples of Toni Morrison's *Beloved* and
      Theresa Hak Kyung Cha's *Dictée*................................... 22

3   Reliving African Matrilineage: Re-Membering
      the Past in Phyllis Alesia Perry's *Stigmata*
      and Gayl Jones's *Corregidora*.. 47

4   Childhood Scars and Women's Love in Emma
      Pérez's *Gulf Dreams* and Paula Gunn Allen's
      The Woman Who Owned the Shadows......................... 79

5   The Case of the Missing Women: Chaos and the
      Absence of Female Bonds in Kathy Acker's Works 106

Conclusion: Resistance and Feminist Healing............. 133

Notes 137

Bibliography 145

Index 155

❉ ACKNOWLEDGMENTS

I would like to express my gratitude to several people who helped in the creation of this project. My sincere thanks is extended to Dr. Lingyan Yang for her guidance and enthusiasm along this journey. My gratitude is also extended to Dr. Susan Comfort and Dr. Veronica Watson for their dedication and direction.

A special thank you goes to Indiana University of Pennsylvania's Dr. Gail Berlin, Chair of the Department of English, and Dr. Yaw Asamoah, Dean of the College of Humanities and Social Sciences, for the generous grant to allow me to complete this book.

Thank you to Christine Pristash and Steven Whitlinger, whose unflagging support and encouragement undoubtedly helped in the creation of this work.

Finally, I also extend my appreciation to the helpful and supportive members of Peter Lang Publishing, particularly Dr. Yoshinobu Hakutani, Series Editor, Caitlin Lavelle, Acquisitions Editor, and Jackie Pavlovic, Production Manager, for their enthusiastic support on this project.

✳ CHAPTER ONE

Introduction: Multiethnic Fragmentation and Women's Community

"We are taught that the body is an ignorant animal; intelligence dwells only in the head. But the body is smart" (Anzaldúa, Borderlands 38).

"[T]he trauma of racism is, for the racists and the victim, the severe fragmentation of the self" (Morrison, "Unspeakable" 16).

"To my daughter Rebecca
Who saw in me
what I considered
a scar
And redefined it
as
a world"
(Walker, Dedication to
In Search of Our Mothers' Gardens*).*

When Victor Frankenstein is asked to create a partner for his hideous and dangerous male monster in Mary Wollstonecraft Shelley's *Frankenstein* (1831), the doctor reluctantly begins the project of creating a female form. However, before the female creature becomes a complete body, Frankenstein decides he cannot, in good conscience, create another being potentially as monstrous as his first creation. Therefore, the voiceless female form is destroyed by the doctor and thrown into the sea while the male monster angrily watches (127). While the scene focuses on the doctor and his male creature, the forgotten female figure remains forever without speech, identity, and subjectivity. She is forever incomplete, a mere collection of fragments that has been envisioned, created, and destroyed at the hands of males. This broken female figure haunts me as I continue to read much later women's writing. In particular, it seems that the incomplete female body is poignantly echoed in multiethnic American women's novels of the mid-1970s through the 1990s. This rich, diverse postmodern literature explores the theme of bodily fragmentation that begins, for women, long before Shelley tackled the issue nearly two centuries ago. What I have noticed is that bodily fragmentation is effectively reflected, in postmodern multiethnic American women's novels, in narrative fragmentation. This fractured, ruptured writing, I believe, suggests a history of fragmented bodies and identities. As Rosi Braidotti argues, "fragmentation" has been "women's historical condition" (121). My goal in this book is to explore how fragmentation has defined women's position in the United States, and how recent, multiethnic American women authors have embraced a disjointed, postmodern writing style both to reflect and to resist their historical state of fragmentation. In many novels, women writers from diverse ethnic and racial heritages, including African American, Asian American, Chicana, Native American, and Jewish American backgrounds, explore wounding and scarring as forms of bodily fragmentation. In these postmodern multiethnic women's novels, the graphic symbols of the wound and scar become manifestations of various forms of oppression. However, these wounds and scars also act as the vehicle through which female characters—across their differences—recognize their shared oppressions, unite in female community, and reclaim their bodies, histories, and identities.

The novels I place into conversation in this analysis are Toni Morrison's *Beloved* (1987), Theresa Hak Kyung Cha's *Dictée* (1982), Phyllis Alesia Perry's *Stigmata* (1999), Gayl Jones's *Corregidora* (1975), Emma Pérez's *Gulf Dreams* (1996), Paula Gunn Allen's *The Woman Who Owned the Shadows* (1983), and Kathy Acker's *Blood and Guts in High School* (1978) and *Empire of the Senseless* (1988). In each of these postmodern, feminist novels, the fragmented female body becomes the means through which women recognize their shared historical wounds and can thus potentially unite in order to resist oppressions caused by patriarchy, racism, and heteronormativity. For example, in *Beloved* and *Dictée*, the female protagonists are connected to their mothers, daughters, and female communities via bodily scars that represent specific, racialized heritages. Sethe's and Beloved's scars connect them to the horrific past of slavery, but furthermore, in their recognition, these same scars eventually connect the women of the community. *Dictée*'s bodily fragmentations represent the ruptures of Korean American identity and of Korea itself, yet they, too, connect daughters and mothers. In *Stigmata* and *Corregidora*, wounds and scars symbolize a haunting reenactment of foremothers' oppressive experiences. The recognition of these (sometimes shared and sometimes differing) experiences, however, allows for connections and resistance. Along comparable lines, *Gulf Dreams* and *The Woman Who Owned the Shadows* celebrate lesbian relationships while the protagonists' fragmented bodies and identities critique the patriarchal, heteronormative societies that condemn them. On the other hand, Acker's novels completely remove the mother and other female companions, and the female protagonists' wounds and scars thus point to a loss of identity devoid of the ability for healing. I examine these eight novels because they work together to generate a similar trajectory for feminist discourse. Their focus on reclaiming the female body and using it as a means of women's (re)connectivity provides a positive feminist direction for women's literature and for women's relationships in general. By examining this set of novels, I wish not to generalize about the authors' or protagonists' experiences, but to suggest that these authors' and protagonists' diverse cultural backgrounds—their race, ethnicity, geography, sexual orientation, class, spirituality/religion—in concert with the novels' focus on bodily and narrative fragmentation—in fact confirm the historical fragmentation of women and demand new forms of writing, female collectivity, and historical memory as means of feminist resistance against patriarchy, racism, and heterosexism.

I pause here to define and clarify some of these terms. This analysis is largely influenced by several feminist theorists, whose collective work informs my definition of "feminism." Importantly, my interest in language and bodily representation reflects my reading of Hélène Cixous, while my focus on corporeality evokes Braidotti and Elizabeth Grosz. Yet my strongest feminist influence is bell hooks, and as I define "feminism" for this study, I begin with her definition. According to hooks, feminism in its most basic form is "the struggle to end sexist oppression" (*Feminist* 26), and I expand this definition to include the unity of women, for only in unity can women overturn patriarchy and end sexist oppression. Hence, feminism, in this study, celebrates women's bonds as means through which oppression can be contested. A "bond," meanwhile, means connection or solidarity. Therefore, "feminist bonds" can include any loving and empowering relationships between women—relationships which undermine patriarchy—including lesbian relationships, friendships, and ties between family members.

Another term I should clarify is "multiethnic," which I use in several ways. First, I define the genre of literature examined in this book as "multiethnic novels" because the grouping of works here emerges from various ethnic and racial backgrounds. Hence the genre itself is classified by multiplicity of race and ethnicity. Moreover, the authors themselves are often products of multiracial, multiethnic, and multicultural backgrounds; their characters, likewise, are often at the crossroads of ethnic and racial identities. Cha's Korean American communities, for example, struggle at the margins of American society, while Allen and her characters are inflected culturally, ethnically, and spiritually by both European and Native American (which itself is a complex and non-homogeneous label) cultures and traditions. Therefore, the authors, their characters, and the genre itself are "multiethnic" on several levels. I choose not to use the term "multiracial" because this term does not necessarily include cultural differences, nor do I use the term "multicultural" because this term does not necessarily attend to diversity of ethnicity. The term "multiethnic," while it still has its own slippages of meaning, includes cultural differences as well as ethnic diversity.

A few other terms should be defined. I use the term "novel" rather loosely in this study, as several of these works of literature (including Cha's *Dictée* and Pérez's *Gulf Dreams*) include elements of autobiography, poetry, and other genres. But this complication of the novel genre only strengthens the study of these works as (postmodern) novels, for the authors challenge and subvert the traditional characteristics of the genre. Thus, they question the idea of "author"itative objectivity, and they reclaim the subjective "I," while moving in a feminist and postmodern direction; one shared characteristic of feminism and postmodernism is, after all, their rigorous challenge to authority and convention. This point begs the question of postmodernism and its definition in this study. The term "postmodern" is used in both a stylistic and a periodizing sense, signifying a group of artistic strategies, including disjointed narrative, shifting perspectives, pastiche, and a challenge to authority, which occurs most frequently in the second half of the twentieth century. I abridge the definition here because this term is defined in depth later in this chapter.

Another key term, "fragmentation," is a purposely broad, umbrella term indicating not only a disjointed style of writing, but also the state of women's bodies, identities, memories, and relationships in a patriarchal era. Examples are the lack of full reproductive rights and the socially compelled competition between women for male approval. These and other fragmentations contribute to a feminized lack of wholeness, and they are often symbolized fictively as bodily fragmentations, or physical wounds, scars, and mutilations. The specific kinds of oppressions that are examined here are patriarchy, racism, and heterosexism. Patriarchy, or rule by the father, manifests itself in various forms, specifically via male dominance within the family, government, church, and other social institutions. Patriarchy is largely maintained and reproduced through heteronormativity, the normalization of heterosexuality, which serves to reproduce the conventional family unit. Heterosexism, then, includes the multitudes of discrimination, mistreatment, and oppression that emerge from heteronormativity. Finally, racism in this study involves the belief in the inherent superiority of the white race; each of the authors presented here critiques the position of "other" that her ethnic group has been forced to assume within American culture. This terminology, given a rather hasty overview here, will be elaborated, deepened, complicated, and clarified throughout this book.

Theoretical approaches for this study include postmodern conceptions of aesthetics, politics, and identities, and feminist theories of embodiment, difference, and sisterhood. Moreover, I problematize issues of race, ethnicity, class, and sexuality. To accomplish these readings, I make use of theoretical lenses provided by Braidotti, hooks, Cixous, Grosz, Gloria Anzaldúa, Trinh Minh-ha, Judith Butler, and Gilles Deleuze and Félix Guattari, among others. Extending from these theorists, I suggest that women's historical fragmentation is reflected in many postmodern, feminist novels, and that bodily wounding and scarring become metaphors for women's historical fragmentation. Moreover, I argue that the symbol of the bodily wound or scar effectively connects women, through its recognition, to their daughters, mothers, grandmothers, lovers, or other women, and suggests sisterhood, matrilineage, and community as potential solutions to historical fragmentation.

In the United States, the twentieth-century proliferation of metaphors such as the "melting pot" and the "cultural mosaic" deceptively advertises a national shift toward inclusiveness. Landmark events such as the success of the Women's Suffrage Movement in 1920 and the Civil Rights Movement of the mid-1950s through the 1970s suggest a move toward acceptance and equality. However, in the late twentieth and early twenty-first century, the increasing economic gap between the wealthy and the poor, the escalated discrimination and racism against immigrant communities, the denial of basic rights to the gay and lesbian community, and the continued debate over women's reproductive rights indicate that inequalities persist. The most harshly victimized, of course, are those who have typically been silenced— the women of racial and ethnic minority groups. For much of the United States' history, white women were denied education, property rights, legal representation, and voting privileges; but for women of racial and ethnic minority groups, these oppressions have been even further escalated. However, despite continued assaults on women's subjectivity and civil liberties, women from diverse backgrounds and histories have found resistant ways of continually challenging the patriarchal status quo politically, academically, socially, and artistically.

The women who represent these experiences through writing, then, must take on the challenge of aesthetically portraying twentieth-century American life from the othered position of the "ethnic" woman. How does one present a history that is rife with struggle, protest, oppression, and resistance? Interestingly, many contemporary, multiethnic women writers often write in purposefully fragmentary ways, taking the modernist style of the early twentieth century as a springboard and reworking it into a uniquely feminist, postmodern voice. Not only does a feminist postmodern style claim a history for these marginalized groups, but it also acts as a tool for resistance and empowerment of multiethnic women. Fractured, disjointed narrative is not new, of course, for the modernists who emerged after World War I rigorously exercised the style of fragmentary narrative. Virginia Woolf, Gertrude Stein, James Joyce, and others challenged the fixed, linear plot of the conventional novel and found new ways of exploring and portraying their worlds. Their unconventional writing was part of a larger social and artistic movement that came to be known as Modernism, which stretched at least until the end of World War II and perhaps through the 1950s.

However, the social and political shifts of the 1960s inaugurated a movement that differed in many ways from the Modernism that characterized the first half of the century. The ability to destroy life on a massive scale—an ability that emerged around World War II—may be one contributing factor in the intellectual and artistic shift. Another may be the social and political upheavals of the mid-1950s through the 1970s. Explanations vary, but theorists tend to agree that Postmodernism, as a movement, emerged in or shortly after the 1940s. For one influential postmodern thinker, Jean-Francois Lyotard, the postmodern is the "incredulity toward metanarratives" (xxiv), or stories defining a culture, and it is World War II that marks a shift toward this "decline of narrative" (37). Another key postmodern theorist, Fredric Jameson, disagrees with Lyotard's "master narrative" theory (*Postmodernism* xi) and suggests instead that postmodernism is "the consumption of sheer commodification as a process" (x). Jameson sees postmodernism as both a periodizing and a stylistic concept, which emerged in late capitalism as a reaction to modernism in the end of the 1950s or the beginning of the 1960s (*Postmodernism* xx). While some disagreement exists about postmodernism's definition and inception, the accepted view is that postmodern thinking and aesthetics were in full swing by the 1960s.

The postmodern era involves some specific artistic and literary shifts. In terms of art and literature, Jameson notes, modernist works by James Joyce and Pablo Picasso are no longer seen as "ugly," but rather, as "realistic" due to their "canonization and academic institutionalization" in the 1950s (*Postmodernism* 4). In other words, modernist art and literature become the rule rather than the exception, with the new generation seeing it as the "establishment" style of their modernist-era parents. Therefore, postmodern art and literature represent a new shift into an era in which, as Jameson notes, art, literature, and architecture acquire "a new depthlessness" and a "weakening of historicity" (*Postmodernism* 6). Similarly, in "Postmodernism and Consumer Society," Jameson notes that postmodernism often involves the "disappearance of a sense of history" and the "fragmentation of time into a series of perpetual presents" ("Postmodernism" 125). This argument suggests that postmodernism lacks a sense of historical connection, and therefore, according to Jameson, postmodernism precludes the possibility for political activism ("Postmodernism" 125).

While Jameson's celebrated studies of postmodern art and society are extraordinarily helpful and thorough, the multiethnic, feminist women authors presented in this study clearly challenge some of his claims. Contrary to what Jameson argues, not only can postmodernism engage with history, but it can also act as a political tool, particularly when combined with feminist concerns. As Ann Bomberger notes in an article on Kathy Acker, postmodern fiction is distinctive not only stylistically for its blending of genres, but also for its blatant "politicism" (189). She points out that postmodern writing "seems to be an easy match with feminism because it engages issues fundamental to feminism: sexuality, political voice, and language's relationship to authority" (189). However, as Bomberger notes, postmodern theorists often doubt that postmodernism can be political "because of capitalism's ability to co-opt and render useless any political attack" (189). Jameson would agree with Bomberger's claim here, but many feminists, including the writers presented in this study, would disagree with

Jameson, embracing postmodernism as a powerful, political, activist, feminist tool. As Ian Gregson notes, Toni Morrison (and I would argue *all* of the writers in this study) "sharply rebukes the depthless, affectless, ahistorical vision of postmodernity" (14).[1] Likewise, as Laurie Vickroy points out, "In order to reveal the effects of slavery through characters' fragmented consciousness and memories, Morrison had to jettison linear or chronological approaches to narrative" (177). And I add, of course, that traumas faced by other characters in these novels also demand the "jettisoning" of conventional narrative structures. Moreover, theorists such as Linda J. Nicholson, Nancy Fraser, and Donna Haraway have successfully argued that feminism and postmodernism are strongly allied. The point here is that a postmodern aesthetic can act as an effective means of feminist, political, and social critique. Certainly, each of the authors discussed in this study creates a fragmented aesthetic style that is uniquely her own but which, in every case, is strongly historicized and political.

As a postmodern strategy, the fragmented novel is embraced by these authors, and it is necessary to delineate what exactly constitutes a fragmented novel. A helpful study by Carol Clark D'Lugo offers one of the most comprehensive explanations of the fragmented novel. Although she discusses only Mexican novels, she so thoroughly defines the fragmented novel as its own genre that I briefly offer here her analysis:

> The most basic definition of a fragmented novel is a work that is broken into sections, with spaces or gaps that separate the pieces of prose. These spaces can be blank or filled with a variety of designs [....][2] Other examples of textual fragmentation are experiments with spacing between words, the repeated use of sentence fragments, and the graphic depiction of disordered thoughts. (xi)

The novels in my study certainly offer these textual "experiments" with spacing, images, and ostensible disorganization. D'Lugo continues by noting that most fragmented novels "follow a basic notion of linearity in that sections are generally read in the normal ordering sequence of first, second, and so on in a syntagmatic arrangement until the end of the novel," but she complicates this idea when she notes that some authors "have further experimented with the ordering of the fragments, offering a choice of reading patterns or refusing any guidance whatsoever" (6). This experimentation is visible in Cha's *Dictée* and in Acker's *Blood and Guts*, when the reader must actively determine, in places, whether to read down the page or to jump back and forth between two pages of alternating text. D'Lugo also says there is often "a haphazard jumping among past, present, and future" (7), and indeed, times overlap in many of the novels in this study, including Perry's *Stigmata*, Jones's *Corregidora*, Pérez's *Gulf Dreams*, and Allen's *The Woman Who Owned the Shadows*. Finally, it is important to mention D'Lugo's belief that fragmentation serves to "destabilize the patriarchy, both in literary and more abstract social terms" (10). Certainly, a primary goal of the novels in my study is to undermine patriarchy, and the writers do so partly by subverting the traditional novel genre. D'Lugo's explanation of the fragmented novel, while it explores only Mexican novels, does provide a helpful description of exactly what constitutes a "fragmented" novel.

The texts discussed here are explicitly postmodern in terms of both their periodization and their stylistic concerns. D'Lugo notes that fragmentation of American novels peaks in the 1960s (187), but this statement marginalizes American (particularly multiethnic) women's writing, in which there is a unique, stylistic fragmentation emerging in the 1970s and continuing through the 1990s. All the novels included in this study were written in the decades of the 1970s, 1980s, and 1990s, with the earliest, Jones's *Corregidora*, published in 1975, and the latest, Perry's *Stigmata*, published in 1999. Historically, this period certainly calls for a resistant form of women's writing. With the conservative backlash following progressive Civil Rights advances of the 1960s and 1970s, women and minorities saw many of their hard-won victories challenged or revoked. Moreover, women saw the stoppage of the Equal Rights Amendment in 1982, a blatant reminder for feminists that their battle continues.

As Acker notes in an interview, "[A]rt and the political processes of the community should be interwoven" ("Apparatus" par. 6). Accordingly, the novels considered here use postmodern aesthetics to narrate specific women's ways of overcoming historical and contemporary oppressions. Though they do so in different ways, each writer in this study uses postmodern narrative that shifts in time, space, and narrative perspective. The polyvocal styles of these authors allow for the perspectives of multiple characters, as opposed to earlier realist or naturalist American novels.[3] Often, the authors criticize Western philosophy itself, which has encouraged belief in the inferior status of women and their bodies. Moreover, contrary to Jameson's claims that postmodern aesthetic lacks a connection to history, these women use their subversive style of writing to reclaim, critique, and celebrate their personal and collective histories. It is helpful here to emphasize that in the United States, women are socialized to compete with one another for male approval. As hooks argues, "Patriarchal thinking normalizes competition" between women (*Communion* 128), and it tells us that "solidarity will never exist between us because we cannot, should not, and do not bond with one another" (*Feminist* 43). This competitive nature, in which women see each other not as partners but as rivals, arises from patriarchy and capitalism, which reinforce heteronormative family structures and which specifically oppress women of ethnic and racial minority groups.[4] In contrast, the writers in this study reclaim and celebrate bonds between women.

The Fragmented Female Body and Feminist Bonds

As the novels in this study show, a postmodern aesthetic is used by many contemporary women writers across ethnicities to reclaim their histories. These women attempt, as Cixous urges, to write in subversive and resistant styles, as they question and challenge the fragmentation of women's bodies and identities through their use of unconventional writing. Minh-ha argues that "[g]athering the fragments of a divided, repressed body and reaching out," and "writing themselves" are ways for women to voice "all that had been silenced in phallocentric discourse" (37). Significantly, each of these postmodern novels contains at least one fragmented female body. The fragmented body is often wounded, scarred, or mutilated in some way, symbolizing a violent history of oppression based on gender, race, ethnicity, class, or sexuality. As Anzaldúa notes, Chicana women are "marked": they are "carved and tattooed with the sharp needles of experience" (*Making* xv). Similarly, Carol E. Henderson's groundbreaking study, *Scarring the Black Body*, which will be looked at more closely in Chapter Three, points out that wounds and scars can appear in many forms, including "decay or disease, mutilation or fragmentation, or textualization in the shared experiences of a community" (114). In other words, the fragmented body itself is not a symbol of resistance or empowerment. Likewise, as Laura Di Prete argues regarding what she calls "corporeal trauma narratives," the body is the "main referent," and the body "in its unquestionable materiality enters these narratives as a visible reminder—not unlike physical scars—of what has been" (14). But these critics raise the question of how women cope with these painful bodily wounds. One solution comes from Ashraf H. A. Rushdy, who notes regarding *Corregidora*'s Ursa that a character can learn to survive oppression not by "making herself a monument to the sufferings of the past," but rather "by healing herself and leaving only the scar tissue and not the open psychic wound as evidence of the horrors of history"

("Relate" 277). Rushdy's somewhat optimistic observations are helpful, but I want to complicate the symbol of the fragmented body further by arguing that these bodily fragmentations, when recognized *by other women*, serve as points of identification and connection. I agree with Butler's observation that the body, while it is socially constructed, is not a passive site of inscription, but rather, is an active and performing agent (*Gender Trouble* 129). Indeed, the multiethnic women in this study find the body to be a text—the site on which historical oppressions are carved, but these women also take an active role in deciphering, sharing, and healing these wounds.

We will see at least a few forms of fragmentation in the coming chapters; examples include the fractured bodies of Sethe and Beloved in *Beloved*, the poetic and actual wounds in *Dictée*, the enslaved and mutilated bodies of Lizzie and Ursa in *Stigmata* and *Corregidora*, the oppressed and fragmented sexualities and bodies of the nameless narrator, the woman from El Pueblo, Ermila, and Ephanie in *Gulf Dreams* and *The Woman Who Owned the Shadows*, and the diseased and destroyed Janey and Abhor in *Blood and Guts* and *Empire*. But, while Elaine Scarry argues that another person's pain is characterized by "unsharability" (4), I believe that the female characters in these novels not only empathetically share each other's pain, but they also understand it to the extent that they can help heal the wounds.[5] The wounds and scars of these characters become symbols of oppression, but more importantly, they offer the potential for recognition, sisterhood, healing, and resistance.

Connections with women allow for the contesting of patriarchy that has fragmented their experiences and bodies. Even though women are socialized to be competitive and to seek male approval, as hooks optimistically notes, women often bond if they have a shared problem (*Communion* 130), and I argue in favor of hooks's concept of "Sisterhood," a bonding between women which "strengthens resistance struggle" (*Feminist* 44). These sisterly connections, in this study, often come in the form of close relationships with mothers, grandmothers, and great-grandmothers. Such matrilineal connection is the case with *Beloved*, *Dictée*, *Stigmata*, and *Corregidora*. The connections also come in the form of relations with other female relatives, such as Lizzie's cousin and aunts in *Stigmata*. Another kind of bond is the complex lesbian relationship between *Gulf Dreams*'s "young woman from El Pueblo" and the novel's narrator, and the relationship between *The Woman Who Owned the Shadows*'s Ephanie and Elena, loving relationships which, due to the heteronormativity underlying each of the characters' respective settings, are unable to come to fruition. These tragically unfulfilled relationships point to the need for bonds between women, and they show the danger of failing to realize those female bonds. Unfulfilled relationships are exacerbated in Acker's works, which demonstrate the chaos and unsustainability of a life entirely bereft of female connection; Acker's works generate a scathing critique of patriarchy through the near-absence of women and the destruction of those present. Acker's male characters may have discovered what Adrienne Rich tellingly notes—that "intense relationships between women in general" are "profoundly threatening to men" (226), and therefore, women's relationships are carefully monitored or destroyed. Therefore, I argue that a new understanding of shared female experience helps women unite in resistance to patriarchy.

As mentioned earlier, the symbol of the fragmented body—marked by the wound, the mutilation, or the scar—often represents historical traumas of a person or community. Yet as Di Prete argues, the traumatized body may also become "the vehicle through which trauma is told and, possibly, worked through" (2). While it is possible to work through these wounds on one's own, I contribute here the additional layer of recognition. Women's recognition of shared wounds often catalyzes the healing process in these novels, for recognition and the resulting bonds between women become the means through which women can heal, and more importantly, can begin to contest those wounds. One example is Amy Tan's *The Joy Luck Club.*[6] When An-mei's mother rubs the scar on An-mei's, neck, it is "as though she were rubbing the memory back into my skin" (38). An-mei notes that women share memories through one another: "It is *shou* [collection] so deep it is in your bones" (41). An-mei believes that forgetting the physical pain that caused the wound allows one to "remember what is in her bones" (41). Below a woman's skin, she believes, is that of her mother, and that of her grandmother, which, if peeled off, leaves a woman with "nothing. No scar, no skin, no flesh" (41). In other words, recalling her matrilineage allows her to overcome the bodily fragmentation she has experienced. This brief example suggests that women can connect through internal memories and experiences, of which scars are the external, recognized symbol.

Within these novels, the body becomes an active agent in remembering history. Cixous's reading of the body provides a helpful inroad. Cixous believes the female body and identity must be won back from the male, arguing, "If she is a whole, it's a whole composed of parts that are wholes" (878)—or a state of perpetual fragmentation. Cixous's belief is that women must write in order to free their bodies from this fragmentary state. One way to do so is to embrace "a *new insurgent* writing" which allows her to reclaim her "rupture[d]" history (880). This new linguistic resistance will enable woman to liberate herself individually and will allow her to make a "shattering entry into history, which has always been based *on her suppression*," in Cixous's words (880). But according to Cixous, with rare exceptions, "there has not yet been any writing that inscribes femininity" (878). While I agree with Cixous's statements about the body's fragmentary state, I also believe that the writers presented in this study *have* discovered a specific, feminist writing style, which they use as a means of subversion and resistance. Their postmodern writing challenges both the conventional novel genre and even some key postmodern theorists. Moreover, their shared literary emphasis on the fragmented body indicates a need for collectivity with other women. Significantly, these relationships are not presented as perfectly harmonious relationships. In fact, these relations are often fraught with what Victoria Burrows calls "the trope of ambivalence" (3), as will be shown. Therefore, I do not wish to portray matrilineal, sisterhood, or female bonds as being without conflict. Rather, I wish to show that the recognition of wounds and scars—as symbols of shared oppression—offer meaningful ways for women to come together in communal resistance.

Overturning Western Philosophical Thought

Beyond the reclamation of history, matrilineage, voice, and subjectivity, the resistant writing these authors employ goes even further. In fact, the narrative style these women use challenges some of the most basic premises of Western philosophical thought. In many cases, these authors describe the "remembering body," or their protagonists physically experience a memory. This bodily memory calls into question the duality between body and mind, which has so dramatically affected philosophical thought in the West. As Christine Everingham notes, feminists have worked to deconstruct the Enlightenment's "key dichotomies of nature/culture and mind/body" (5). Everingham points out that these culturally engrained dichotomies "have been shown to enhance men's emancipation at the expense of constraining women's" because these concepts are portrayed as "mutually exclusive and opposing categories" (6). Everingham is correct to note that feminists have questioned these dichotomies, and the authors in this study certainly do likewise. Particularly problematic to these authors is the perceived split between the mind and body, because this dichotomy prohibits a holistic understanding of identity. Of course, physicality is integral to and inextricable from identity; therefore, the protagonists of these novels endure historical oppressions that affect them in the form of bodily wounds, mutilations, and scars—corporeal fragmentations that equally affect mind and body (and all other elements of selfhood).

By criticizing the mind/body duality, these authors challenge the very basis of Western thought—that of dualism. To support this claim, a brief overview of the Western philosophical division between body and mind is necessary.[7] When Plato tells the allegory of the cave in his *Republic*, he gives an image to the division between body and spirit that he imagines (7.518). Moreover, this binary becomes hierarchized—with one half privileged—because Plato crystallizes the division between light/soul/knowledge/goodness and those things that are perceived to be their opposites: darkness/body/ignorance/evil (7.518). These divisions have developed distinct associations with gender (male and female), race, (white and "other"), and sexuality (heterosexual and LGBTQ). Continuing this philosophical tradition, Aristotle's influential thinking characterizes male and female as diametrically opposed (and certainly hierarchized) beings. He notes in "The Generation of Animals" that women are "weaker and colder in nature," as opposed to man's stronger, warmer nature (4.6). Men are the active agents, while women are the passive recipients (4.2), and men are characterized by "capacity," while women, "incapacity" (4.1). Ultimately, according to Aristotle, "we must look upon the female character as being a sort of natural deficiency" (4.6). These early philosophers succeed not only in creating a lasting division between body and mind, but in linking this division to our very identities as women and men.

Later, Descartes connects these binaries to existence itself, separating the soul from nature by distinguishing two types of substances, an intellectual substance (the mind) and an extended substance (the body). These two substances are part of a dualistic system in which mind and body are distinct and separable, and in which mind is privileged over body ("Sixth Meditation"). According to corporeal feminist Elizabeth Grosz, "Descartes, in short, succeeded in linking the mind/body opposition to the foundations of knowledge itself, a link which places the mind in a position of hierarchical superiority over and above nature, including the nature of the body" (6). This concept has become a staple of Western thought, constituting our identities in the twenty-first century as a natural part of human existence. The Christian tradition, of course, has only perpetuated these binaries, linking the soul to purity and salvation, and the body to sin and damnation. Because women are more closely associated with the body vis-à-vis these binaries, they are perceived as more connected to the natural world and to the "lower" functions of the body. They are viewed as more nurturing, since their bodies prepare them for childbearing, and as less capable of higher orders of thinking, which Jacques Derrida points out are associated with the phallus or *logos* (81). Unfortunately, as Grosz observes, three hundred years of philosophy have yet to overturn the dualisms that Descartes has instituted (6).

However, as French phenomenologist Maurice Merleau-Ponty points out, the body is the necessary vehicle through which we experience the world, and bodily and psychological processes are therefore inextricable from and necessary to one another (29). As I argue later, many of the authors in this study, including Cha, Perry, Pérez, and Allen, subversively use Christian elements, particularly those of the Roman Catholic tradition, to critique the body/mind split and the denigration of the body (particularly the female body and female sexuality). Moreover, all of the authors in this study challenge Plato, Aristotle, and Descartes by generating remembering or re-membered bodies. These bodies demonstrate that the psychological processes of the mind are inseparable from the body's responses. This reconnection of body and mind not only calls for a re-evaluation of the body, but it also deconstructs the foundational binaries of Western philosophy, upon which many forms of oppression are based.

Summary of Chapters

The novels selected for this study connect postmodern, feminist, fragmented writing with poignant depictions of the fragmented female body. The novels are paired thematically such that each chapter discusses two novels entailing similar concerns, though the major concern is always the eradication of sexist oppression, to paraphrase hooks's definition of feminism (*Feminist* 26). Before I begin the detailed chapter summaries, I clarify the book's organizational rationale. In the second chapter, the novels entail discussions of mother/daughter bonds. Relationships between mother and child, as we will observe, are often complex and troubled, yet they are generally the initial relationship formed by a human being. Hence, I begin with this most primary of relationships as a springboard for exploring many kinds of female bonds. The third chapter moves further into matrilineage by exploring relationships not only with mothers, but also with grandmothers, great-grandmothers, and great-great-grandmothers. Thus, the scope of feminist bonds becomes more deeply ancestral in this chapter. This third chapter closes with the protagonists' overturning of the convention of childbearing, a useful segue into the fourth chapter, which expands these concerns to examine the heteronormative demand for specific familial structures. This fourth chapter investigates lesbian relationships and critiques the heteronormative structures that devalue them. The novels in this chapter suggest alternatives to "traditional" families and encourage social acceptance of "othered" forms of female bonds, though we see the trauma resulting from women's inability to maintain bonds. And finally, the study leaves us, in the fifth chapter, with the prospect of having no female bonds whatsoever. Hence, the trajectory of the study moves from original mother/daughter bonds to foremothers' bonds to "other/ed" women's bonds (which are precluded by society) to no women's bonds whatsoever. Likewise, it also moves from the matriarchal families of Sethe, Denver, and Beloved, and Theresa and Hyung Soon Huo (Cha's mother), to Janey Smith's and Abhor's entirely patriarchal families (fathers Johnny and Bud are extremely abusive). The goal of this organization is to expand women's feminist bonds from the original mother/child relationship outwards to include all forms of women's bonds.

Chapter Two, "The Fragmented Body and Maternal Healing: The Examples of Toni Morrison's *Beloved* and Theresa Hak Kyung Cha's *Dictée*," connects two novels that entail similar thematic concerns. These two novels present the experiences of diasporic communities, Cha's focusing on the Korean colonial and immigrant experience and Morrison's on the African American experience during and after slavery. Both novels are strongly resistant, and both present the empowerment provided by matrilineal bonds in an ethnic American community. Both celebrate and complicate matrilineal bonds, and they each find a means of contesting historical fragmentation via these and other women's bonds. Morrison's *Beloved* acts as both a springboard for this chapter and a model for the entire study. Although much scholarship exists on this brilliant, award-winning novel, *Beloved*'s emphasis on bodily fragmentation and communal healing gives it a prominent place in my study. Sethe's and Beloved's scars in particular show that the experiences of the past have left a visible, physical presence on the characters' present identities. Yet it is female community in particular that helps each of these wounded characters to heal. Exploring some parallel concerns, Cha's *Dictée* critiques dominant patriarchal and militaristic histories. This nonlinear novel is highly fragmented with short stories, autobiographical sketches, photographs, ideographs, poetry, diagrams, charts, and maps, yet it is held together as a cohesive novel by its consistent themes and by the inextricability of any one chapter from the whole. In every section, Cha criticizes the masculine, militaristic episodes that take primacy in written history, specifically the Japanese colonization of Korea. Like *Beloved*, *Dictée* urges women's bonds, particularly those with one's mother, as a means of contesting these histories.

Chapter Three, "Reliving African Matrilineage: Re-Membering the Past in Phyllis Alesia Perry's *Stigmata* and Gayl Jones's *Corregidora*," focuses on the reclamation of foremothers' history through its literal inscription on the contemporary female body. The protagonists of each novel experience physically and psychologically the events of their foremothers' histories of enslavement and oppression. Perry's *Stigmata* tells the story of Lizzie DuBose, a young woman living in the 1990s, who begins experiencing her great-great-grandmother's and grandmother's histories. We learn that her foremothers' painful experiences are being revisited upon their granddaughters' bodies so that their stories can be re-"membered." In order to heal, Lizzie's primary goal is to reclaim Sarah, who is both her mother and her daughter; this recognition, Lizzie believes, will help her heal and allow the cycle to end. Similarly, *Corregidora*'s protagonist, Ursa Corregidora, a lounge singer in the 1940s through the 1960s, has been told the stories of her enslaved and oppressed foremothers (great-grandmother and grandmother) so thoroughly that she experiences their histories as her own. The kind of memory Lizzie and Ursa experience is similar to the concept of "rememory" that Toni Morrison introduces in *Beloved* (36), but Jones's version appears thus: "It was as if their memory, the memory of all the Corregidora women, was her memory too, as strong with her as her own private memory, or almost as strong" (129). But when Ursa falls down a flight of stairs in the novel's first pages, she loses her uterus and the familial mandate to "make generations" who will carry on this story. This chapter shows how Ursa and Lizzie must contend with their painful matrilineal histories, reconnect with their mothers, and find new ways of survival in the twentieth century.

Chapter Four, "Childhood Scars and Women's Love in Emma Pérez's *Gulf Dreams* and Paula Gunn Allen's *The Woman Who Owned the Shadows*," critiques the patriarchal, heteronormative societies that preclude loving relationships in these two novels. *Gulf Dreams* follows the love between an unnamed narrator and her unnamed lover, the young woman from El Pueblo, while *The Woman Who Owned the Shadows* explores the childhood connection between protagonist Ephanie, a Native American girl, and Elena, a Chicana girl. Both novels are fragmented chronologically, involving a series of vignettes that jump from past to present and from dreams to reality. Unlike *Stigmata* and *Corregidora*, these two novels do not explore the recovery and perpetuation of matrilineal history. Instead, they focus on romantic relationships with other girls/women, relationships which are destroyed in a heteronormative world. Indeed, in both novels, normative male-female relationships and the structures that come with them (familial, religious, and social) compel the protagonists' female lovers to abandon them. Moreover, both novels portray fragmented bodies—particularly in *Gulf Dreams*'s fight scene, the story of Ermila's rape, and *The Woman Who Owned the Shadows*'s life-changing fall from the apple tree—as symbols of the destructive confines of heteronormative society. The fragmented memories, chronologies, and bodies within these two novels both represent and critique the fragmentation caused by patriarchal and heteronormative regimes. However, these novels also portray the resistance and completeness that can potentially arise from strong relationships between women.

Finally, Chapter Five, "The Case of the Missing Women: Chaos and the Absence of Female Bonds in Kathy Acker's Works," examines two novels by Acker, a feminist, postmodern, Jewish American (though she does not claim this ethnic heritage) author who uses extreme narrative fragmentation to expose the historical fragmentation of the female body and identity. Acker's works are so fragmented and so incisively critical of patriarchy that two of them are examined in this final chapter. In *Blood and Guts*, the protagonist, ten-year-old Janey Smith, whose mother dies when Janey is a year old, is raised by her abusive, incestuous father. This problematic relationship leads to a series of painful relationships between Janey and violent, patriarchal men. In *Empire*, the novel shifts in time and space and between the perspectives of the "black female cyborg," Abhor, and Thivai, a young male character. Abhor's mother also dies early, and Abhor is, like Janey, raped by her father. Interestingly, both female protagonists are entirely without female friends and community. This lack of female bonds leads to chaos and shifting identities, and the bodies of Janey and Abhor are severely fragmented in the process—Janey, for example, is diseased and maimed by her sexual relations with abusive men, and Abhor is violently sliced by her male companions. This chapter does not intend to suggest that a mother's presence is necessary in order for a stable identity to be discovered. Rather, the chapter suggests that Acker's novels, in particular, emphasize maternal bonds and other forms of female connection as a viable means for contesting patriarchal power, which is dangerously rampant in these two novels.

By pairing these works in individual chapters and placing them as a whole into conversation with one another, I realize the danger in my claims. I hope not to affirm any type of "traditional," mother-father relationship, nor the idea of conventional motherhood, nor the notion of maternalism, nor even the necessity of a mother in the biological or adoptive sense of the word. Nor, of course, do I oppose these relationships. I am also not arguing that these novels are meant to fit into what Madhu Dubey calls the "matrilineage paradigm," which involves an "idealized" and "uncritical preoccupation with the mother's past" (253). Dubey points out that Jones's *Corregidora*, for example, does not fit this paradigm, and I argue, in fact, that none of the novels in this study fits, because each novel, as Dubey insists *Corregidora* does, "pluralizes the past" (253). These novels all envision a solidarity between women, but they are also fraught with complexity, pain, and ambivalence, and they show the difficulty of each woman's unique history. I also do not wish to suggest that women should devalue meaningful relationships with men. The claim I am making here is not meant to suggest that fathers, grandfathers, and male partners are insignificant to these women or to the novels, and in fact, many of these women have strong and meaningful connections with men. Rather, I am suggesting that these novels use specifically female bonds to contest not individual men or even men in general, but patriarchy as a larger construct.

A few more caveats are necessary here. Importantly, I do not assume a heterosexual, nuclear family structure, nor do I privilege any one type of familial structure over another. To insist on any type of relationship would be to claim that one model fits the lives of every woman in every time and place. In fact, I am not passing any sort of judgment whatsoever on any particular form of relationship—many of which (including multitudes of other relational styles not mentioned here) can provide meaningful and loving spaces for growth, expression, and compassion. Therefore, I hope this study is not interpreted to favor one form of relationship over another—a judgment which would in fact contradict this study's intention. Rather, I hope to indicate that women's bonds—conventional or unconventional, physical, spiritual, emotional, intellectual, or otherwise—are shown, in these American multiethnic women's novels, to be viable ways of healing and of resisting patriarchal constraints. With this being said, I also do not suggest that women are more connected to children, or that they are more easily bonded to one another, or that they are somehow more capable of forming attachments or feeling compassion in general, than are men. To do so would suggest a biological essentialism that defines women as "naturally" more emotional, nurturing, compassionate, and even dependent than men. On the contrary, this study examines women's bonds as the literary antidote to social, historical, and political oppressions specific to women of multiethnic groups. Importantly, I reject the idea of "common oppression," an idea which undermines the "true nature of women's varied and complex social reality" (hooks, *Feminist* 44). The bonds I suggest arise out of wounds shared between specific women, and those wounds are unique and complex.

Finally, I do not wish to create a monolithic view of what women's fragmented novels "mean," or what the female body, the wound, or the scar might symbolize. I also do not argue that the characters in these novels are resigned to an oppressed or fragmentary state. Instead, I argue that these specific, resistant novels celebrate matrilineage and sisterhood through the healing of shared cultural wounds and fragmented histories. As Grosz states, "Bodies have all the explanatory power of minds" (vii). I want to suggest that the bodies of the women presented in these novels are presented as physical reminders of an individual and collective history of oppression that, in particular, women of ethnic minority groups in the United States have resisted.

(Re)Writing History

In Cristina García's *Dreaming in Cuban*, Pilar Puente quickly learns that history is innately biased toward a male, militaristic point of view. She recalls the stories her father told her, stories involving Christopher Columbus and European conquests. Pilar notes that history books are "always one damn battle after another," and that schools teach Charlemagne and Napoleon "because they *fought* their way into posterity" (28). The female perspective is missing in many historical accounts, so Pilar wishes to celebrate the female voice and experience. "If it were up to me, I'd record other things," says Pilar; "Like the time there was a freak hailstorm in the Congo and the women took it as a sign that they should rule. Or the life stories of prostitutes in Bombay. Why don't I know anything about them?" (28). She sees that female experiences are not as important to written history as are conquests by men. The problem is summed up when Pilar asks, "Who chooses what we should know or what's important?" (28). She sees that choices are consciously made, and that specific histories are purposely devalued. Postmodern scholars Mas'ud Zavarzadeh and Donald Morton agree, noting that what is read and believed as history is a large system of ideas produced and maintained by those in power, ideas which exclude certain histories in order to perpetuate dominant ideologies (54). In this way, history must be understood as "a contestation of diverse textualizations" and not as a "solid" and fixed narrative (54). Zavarzadeh and Morton argue, "It is necessary [...] to combat the dominant ideology because it foreshortens the horizon of historical possibilities by constructing the world in terms that legitimate the interests of one class by subjugating others" (16). Indeed, history has erased the stories of many, an exclusion which may explain why Lizzie DuBose and Ursa Corregidora must physically relive their histories. Because of this erasure, as Minh-ha argues, "the re-writing of history is therefore an endless task [....] The more they [feminist scholars] dig into the maze of yellowed documents and look into the non-registered facts of their communities, the more they rejoice upon discovering the buried treasures of women's unknown heritage" (84). In other words, it is extremely important to find new ways of recording history and sharing stories. Certainly, the writing styles of the authors in this study, as well as the experiences of the protagonists, generate new ways of remembering history.

As I move into my analysis of the interconnections between fragmented narrative, fragmented bodies, women's recognition of shared wounds, and female community, I reflect on Victor Frankenstein's aborted female creature. If she had come into existence, I wonder, what would her life have been like? Without the community and matrilineal heritage of Sethe, Theresa, Lizzie, and Ursa, how would she understand her existence? Would the possibility of love be foreclosed, as it is for the young woman from El Pueblo, the nameless narrator, Ephanie, and Elena? Or would her sense of self be entirely shattered, as is the case with Janey and Abhor? Without others like her, surely the female creature would have no way of understanding her very literally fragmented, pieced-together body. Likewise, the authors in this study seem to suggest that women who share in each other's experiences can begin to resist and to heal.

❋ CHAPTER TWO

The Fragmented Body and Maternal Healing: The Examples of Toni Morrison's *Beloved* and Theresa Hak Kyung Cha's *Dictée*

"Wounds, misshapen bodies, scarred or marked flesh always tell a story through their opening onto the world" (Slattery 14).

"In women there is always more or less of the mother who makes everything all right, who nourishes, and who stands up against separation" (Cixous 882).

The 1980s proved an especially fruitful time for women's experimental writing. Significantly, the emergence of this writing coincides with the Reagan administration and the backlash against progressive 1960s and 1970s advances in civil rights. The Equal Rights Amendment was quashed in 1982, as American culture gravitated back toward more socially conservative ideas. In response to this retreat into social and political conservatism, women of ethnic and racial minorities began to speak, write, and protest more loudly than ever before. The roots of what Alice Walker has termed "Womanism," a movement devoted to the uplift and celebration of women of all races, ethnicities, classes, and sexual orientations (*In Search* xi), began to take root in the United States. From this historical context emerge the two novels that are the focus of this chapter: African American author Toni Morrison's renowned *Beloved* (1987) and Korean American author Theresa Hak Kyung Cha's *Dictée* (1982). Morrison and Cha present highly fragmented novels that use polyvocal, disjointed narrative styles. Moreover, these two novelists similarly critique patriarchy by celebrating individual and cultural matrilineage. Both *Dictée* and *Beloved* examine the fragmented female body and its connections to historical oppressions, and ultimately, they both portray how maternal recognition and feminist, communal bonds are potential ways of beginning the healing process.

While both novels provide powerful criticisms of patriarchy and racism, *Dictée* specifically critiques the Japanese colonizing of Korea, while *Beloved* focuses on oppression during and after institutionalized American slavery. Despite their significant differences, both novels present feminist critiques of patriarchy's hold on social, cultural, and familial structures. Moreover, both novels encourage the discovery of matrilineal and communal bonds to overturn these power structures, while celebrating a feminist, resistant form of healing.

Toni Morrison's *Beloved*

Morrison's celebrated fifth novel, *Beloved*, provides a comprehensive point of departure for this study: It emphasizes bodily fragmentation caused by historical oppressions, and it exemplifies the healing powers of feminist bonds. Morrison's impressive literary and academic accomplishments begin in 1930s Ohio, where she grew up. Many of her novels are consequently set in Ohio, as is the case with *Beloved*. Becoming the first African American to win the Nobel Prize in Literature with *Beloved*, Morrison's prodigious record of literature and criticism continues into the twenty-first century. Her concern with the intersections between race, gender, and class, injected with profound accounts of history, remains her cornerstone. *Beloved*, which is dedicated to the "Sixty Million and more" who died along the Middle Passage, has been the subject of vast amounts of criticism;[8] therefore, my study distinguishes itself by connecting the fragmentation of narrative and body to the call for female community as a form of healing and resistance. It also distinguishes itself by joining a conversation with *Dictée*. Ultimately, my discussion provides a postmodern feminist link between text, body, women's relationships, and healing.

Beloved emphasizes the tragic legacy of slavery and the importance of cultural memory; to do so, it explores multiple forms of fragmentation: bodily, cultural, sexual, and racial. Significantly, the novel uses a masterful and powerful narrative fragmentation. The novel is told from the perspectives of numerous characters, including the profoundly fragmentary and traumatized voice of Beloved herself. The chapters are generally narrated from a third-person, limited-omniscient viewpoint, telling the experiences of Sethe or Denver, for example, though several chapters allow for first-person accounts, specifically Beloved's two poignant and haunting chapters. In each chapter, we learn details of Sethe's history at Sweet Home and at 124 Bluestone Road, Cincinnati, as well as the stories of Baby Suggs (Sethe's mother-in-law), Paul D and the other Sweet Home men, Stamp Paid, Denver, and Beloved. This polyvocal method of telling, according to Ashraf H. A. Rushdy, exemplifies Henry Louis Gates, Jr.'s "speakerly texts" (Rushdy, "Daughters" 586), which Gates defines as texts that "imitat[e] one of the numerous forms of oral narration to be found in classical Afro-American vernacular literature" (Gates 181). The telling of each chapter is much like an oral transmission in which elements of a story are emphasized, repeated, implied, or omitted. Rushdy notes further that this form of narration becomes "the site of an oral history passed from generation to generation" ("Daughters" 587). This statement helps theorize the fragmentary telling of *Beloved*. Sethe, for example, transmits her story as an oral narrative, which Denver then enhances and tells Beloved. However, I want to add to Rushdy's argument by pairing this kind of textual transmission to the fragmented bodies of the characters. I suggest further that it is also corporeally that these stories are transmitted.

Fragmentation and Healing in *Beloved*

To transmit these stories between characters, Morrison employs the image of the scar, a symbol for the trauma of the past. Corporeal scars are visible on many characters, including major characters Beloved and Sethe as well as minor characters such as Ella (258) and Sethe's mother (61). Most obviously, Beloved's scar on her neck reveals her identity as the daughter murdered by Sethe. Sethe, of course, wants to protect Beloved from the atrocities of slavery and thus kills her—a story based on the actual events of Margaret Garner's life.[9] Therefore, Beloved's scar is symbolic both in its connection to the bodily and emotional wounds of slavery's past and in its connection to matrilineal history. Likewise, Sethe bears horrific scars on her back as a result of her torture at the ironically-named Sweet Home plantation. Both Beloved's and Sethe's highly symbolic scars serve to connect characters whose lives have been fragmented by the trauma of slavery. I should also point out that *Beloved* portrays both the wound and the scar. The distinction is important since the scar—the healed form of the wound—demonstrates how female bonds are capable of healing historical oppressions (if not removing their lasting effects). As Laurie Vickroy points out, "Characters' scars become both connecting points and obstacles to potentially intimate or sexual relations, drawing others' sympathy" (32). Vickroy believes that when Paul D kisses Sethe's back, he is essentially saying, "I share these wounds" (183)—though I would point out that they are scars.   Indeed, the central male character, Paul D, also bears the psychic/physical effects of his past and recognizes this suffering in other men and women; however, it is women specifically who carry bodily scars indicative of their particular, gendered abuses.[10]   Moreover, these wounds and scars are fully recognized only by other women, in whose community the process of healing can begin.

Sethe herself is horrifically fragmented by the institution of slavery.   In addition to the fractured identity and painful dehumanization caused by her enslavement, Sethe is sexually abused by schoolteacher and his two nephews at Sweet Home, a small plantation owned by the Garners and worked by Sethe, Paul A, Paul D, Paul F, Sixo, and Halle (Sethe's husband).   As Sethe says to Paul D, "[T]hose boys came in there and took my milk [....] Held me down and took it" (16).   This sexual fragmentation is of utmost significance to Sethe, who repeats that "they took my milk" while Paul D is more enraged that they have beaten a pregnant woman (17).   After this traumatic event, which drives Sethe's husband to insanity (Halle is last seen sitting by the churn smearing butter on his face), Sethe tells her mistress, Mrs. Garner, what these men have done to her.   When the men discover that Sethe has complained about them, schoolteacher orders one of his nephews to whip Sethe (16).   The wounds caused by this punishment create the "chokecherry tree" Sethe describes, a tree that "grows there still" (16).   It is significant to note that the wounds created by the whipping have healed, or "closed" (17), but the fact that the tree "grows there still" indicates ongoing trauma.

Shortly after Sethe's escape, Amy Denver discovers her, and in her willingness to heal, Amy provides a striking example of feminist solidarity. It is Amy, a young white woman headed for Boston, who cares for Sethe, delivers Denver, and significantly, names Sethe's wounds:

It's a tree, Lu [the alias Sethe quickly chooses when she is discovered].   A chokecherry tree. See, here's the trunk—it's red and split wide open, full of sap, and this here's the parting for the branches. You got a mighty lot of branches. Leaves, too, look like, and dern if these ain't blossoms. Tiny little cherry blossoms, just as white. Your back got a whole tree on it. In bloom. What God have in mind, I wonder. (79)

Not only does she recognize Sethe's wounds, but she shares some level of understanding: "I had me some whippings, but I don't remember nothing like this" (79). Although she is in a far safer social position as a white woman (and her goal is to buy velvet, not to escape slavery), Amy sympathizes with Sethe's wounds. I agree with bell hooks here; there is surely no "common oppression" between these two women (*Feminist* 44). Yet there is a recognition of wounds that provides the impetus for sisterhood and healing. Despite Sethe's sickening appearance, Amy courageously wonders, "Maybe I ought to break them blossoms open. Get that pus to running, you think?" (80). She remains with Sethe and in fact begins healing Sethe's bodily wounds by rubbing her feet back to life, spreading cobwebs on her back, and eventually delivering a three-month-premature Denver (79-80). Amy Denver's steadfastness in the face of this horrific and gory scene provides a strong testament to sisterhood and its healing power.

Likewise, when Sethe arrives at 124, her mother-in-law, Baby Suggs, must contend with the horror of Sethe's experiences:

> Sethe dozed and woke to the washing of her hands and arms. After each bathing, Baby covered her with a quilt and put another pan on in the kitchen. Tearing sheets, stitching the gray cotton [....] When Sethe's legs were done, Baby looked at her feet and wiped them lightly. She cleaned between Sethe's legs with two separate pans of hot water and then tied her stomach and vagina with sheets. Finally she attacked the unrecognizable feet. (93)

Like Amy Denver, Baby Suggs must maintain composure despite such a horrific scene. It is Sethe's back that is most traumatic to each caretaker, for when Baby Suggs sees that "[r]oses of blood blossomed in the blanket covering Sethe's shoulders," Baby "hid her mouth with her hand," and "wordlessly" she "greased the flowering back and pinned a double thickness of cloth to the inside of the newly stitched dress" (93). Like Amy Denver, Baby Suggs takes on the most gruesome of tasks to help Sethe heal. But Baby Suggs's silence, opposed to Amy's cheerful chatter, may signify a deeper understanding. Having experienced slavery and Sweet Home herself, Baby Suggs is a more empathetic person. These distinctions, however, only strengthen *Beloved*'s call for sisterhood, for they emphasize that women can unite across differences. Indeed, Sethe's decision to name her daughter after the white woman, despite Sethe's traumatic life of enslavement by whites, signifies her own acceptance of feminist bonds. Hence, both Baby Suggs and Amy Denver stand as powerful examples of sisterhood and feminist healing.

When the reader meets Sethe, it is eighteen years after this event, and the wounds have since healed. Their legacy, however, is still visible on Sethe's skin, and certainly, the effects linger in Sethe's memory. The image of the scar, then, metonymically represents Sethe's ongoing trauma. Yet the scar is not solely a marker of trauma and devastation. It is certainly not positive in any way, but as Dennis Patrick Slattery appropriately notes, "To retrieve one's own embodiment, bit by bit and piece by piece, and to stitch the parts back together is at the same time to reclaim the history of that embodiment" (212). In other words, as Sethe heals, she also reclaims her own body and history. The scars in fact provide resistance and hope, for they indicate that, although the physical and psychological effects remain, the process of healing has begun.

Following Amy Denver's and Baby Suggs's attention to Sethe's open wounds, the first person to sympathize with these wounds *after* they have healed into scars is Paul D: "[S]he felt Paul D behind her [....] and knew, but could not feel, that his cheek was pressing into the branches of her chokecherry tree" (17). He silently suggests his sorrow, understanding, and connection to Sethe's experiences, and he opens her dress to view the scars: "He rubbed his cheek on her back and learned that way her sorrow, the roots of it; its wide trunk and intricate branches" (17). Unfortunately, after a brief and unsatisfying trip to Sethe's bedroom, Paul D suddenly becomes revolted by Sethe's body: "Out of the corner of his eye, Paul D saw the float of her breasts and disliked it, the spread-away, flat roundness of them that he could definitely live without" (21). More problematic, however, is the fact that Paul D becomes suddenly disgusted by Sethe's scars, with which, moments ago, he had seemed to empathize: The "maze" he had caressed in the kitchen "was in fact a revolting clump of scars. Not a tree, as she said. Maybe shaped like one, but nothing like any tree he knew because trees were inviting; things you could trust and be near" (21). Thus, even though Paul D actually shares some of Sethe's experiences from Sweet Home, he is still unable to move beyond his revulsion toward a complete understanding of Sethe's wounds. He has suffered his own traumatic experiences, but some of the specific abuses Sethe has endured, many of them gendered, are perhaps what precludes full male-female empathy. Paul D's failure to recognize and empathize effectively proscribes his own ability to help Sethe's healing process. His disgust is contrasted with Amy Denver's and Baby Suggs's willingness to help. Indeed, the wounds are so horrific that even a man of Paul D's unspeakable experiences is repelled years later by the scars (not the far worse open wounds that Amy and Baby behold), and it is thus women across race and ethnicity who must provide the means of healing.

The other important scars in the novel, of course, belong to Beloved. Of Sethe's four children, only Denver remains at 124 (Howard and Buglar run away)—along with the ghost of the baby whom Sethe killed twenty-eight days after beginning a new, free life in Cincinnati. After Paul D drives the ghost out of the house, a young woman appears on the tree stump when Sethe, Paul D, and Denver return from the carnival. Although Sethe does not immediately realize that the young woman is indeed her (re)incarnated daughter, Denver does. Denver's realization may come from her physical connection to her sister's wounds, for when Beloved is killed, Denver is nursed shortly thereafter, and she swallows "her mother's milk right along with the blood of her sister" (152). Eighteen years later, Denver's recognition of her sister is only confirmed by "the tip of the thing she saw when Beloved lay down or came undone in her sleep" (120). This scar, visible to Denver, is not seen by Sethe until later, when she spies "the little curved shadow of a smile in the kootchy-kootchy-coo place under the chin" (239). Moreover, if this scar were not enough proof, Beloved has three small scars, "three vertical scratches" (51), on her forehead where her mother held her head up as she bled to death (203). In other words, these visible, physical markers of Beloved's past are what prove her identity. Sethe's recognition of these scars catalyzes her explanations of why she murdered the infant, and through her words, Sethe hopes to heal the damage that has been done. Beloved's corporeal scars indicate her identity, they suggest the historical legacy of slavery, and they provide Sethe with the impetus to try to heal Beloved.

Also relevant here is that Beloved seems very conscious that she was physically destroyed in the past and that she is still vulnerable. Beloved fears that she will either explode or be swallowed (133), fears which Naomi Morgenstern persuasively connects: "The infant's experience of the precariousness of self-image [...] resonates with the slave's experience of a fragmented body, a body that belongs to someone else" (114-15). This fear becomes evident when Beloved pulls out a tooth:

> This is it. Next would be her arm, her hand, a toe. Pieces of her would drop maybe one at a time, maybe all at once. Or on one of those mornings before Denver woke and after Sethe left she would fly apart. It is difficult keeping her head on her neck, her legs attached to her hips when she is by herself. Among the things she could not remember was when she first knew that she could wake up any day and find herself

in pieces [....] When her tooth came out—an odd fragment, last in the row—she thought it was starting. (133)

Like the lack of control experienced by enslaved people, Beloved, too, feels that she is not in control of her own body. Of course, Sethe's rationale for Beloved's murder is that the damage of slavery is worse, and due to her corporeal destruction caused by slavery and by her mother, Beloved is constantly aware of her precarious, fragmentary state. Beloved's uncertain existence as a reincarnated being, however, also suggests her status as a sort of open wound. Her body threatens to fall apart all at once, yet in an inversion of power, Beloved begins to grow grotesquely larger; as she grows, much like a painful wound, she becomes more damaging to Sethe. Hence, Beloved comes to symbolize the wounds of slavery, and eventually, she herself must be driven out, or healed, by the women of the community.

It is vital to recall that the wounds in this study are certainly not positive in any sense. Wounds are, in most cases, the symbol of racial and gendered oppression. However, the *recognition* of wounds, scars, or other marks provides the impetus to begin healing. To be sure that wounds and scars are not construed in a positive light, Morrison includes the example of Sethe's mother, whom Sethe barely knows. Sethe learns that her mother has been branded, a particularly dehumanizing form of corporeal fragmentation that indicates her status as a commodity:

[S]he opened up her dress front and lifted her breast and pointed under it. Right on her rib was a circle and a cross burnt right into the skin. She said, "This is your ma'am. This," and she pointed. "I am the only one got this mark now. The rest dead. If something happens to me and you can't tell me by my face, you can know me by this mark." Scared me so. All I could think of was how important this was and how I needed to have something important to say back, but I couldn't think of anything so I just said what I thought. "Yes, Ma'am," I said. "But how will you know me? How will you know me? Mark me, too," I said. "Mark the mark on me too." (61)

Sethe sees this mark as a symbol of maternal recognition, a point echoed by Slattery, who notes that the scar becomes a "bond, knitting together rather than separating mother and daughter" (218). Yet when Sethe asks for a similar mark, her mother slaps her (61). As Sethe says, "I didn't understand it then. Not till I had a mark of my own" (61). The horrified response by Sethe's mother to this question indicates that a brand, scar, or wound imposed by another person is an exercise of control. Regardless, a younger Sethe wishes to share in the wounds of her mother so that she and her mother are recognizable to one another. Lucille P. Fultz examines this scene, noting that Sethe's mother "makes herself known to Sethe by the cruel hieroglyphics on her body" (37). Fultz acknowledges that Sethe's misunderstanding of the mark leads her to ask "for some recognizable bond between herself and her mother" (37). Interestingly, now that Sethe has "a mark of my own" in the form of her own scars, she "understand[s]" her mother's reaction (Morrison, *Beloved* 61). It is this understanding that is at the heart of this study, for wounds and scars are symbols of a traumatic past, but the understanding that arises out of these visual markers provides a beginning site for healing and resistance.

By focusing on the physical and psychological repercussions of slavery and showing their inextricability from one another, *Beloved* contests the traditional Western split between mind and body. Sethe's corporeal scars are representations of the psychological trauma she undergoes, and that her tree "grows there still" indicates the memories' ongoing presence (16). Moreover, as outlined in the Introduction, Western philosophy binaries privilege the half aligned with the spirit or mind. On the contrary, *Beloved* emphasizes the centrality of the body. Beloved's return first as a spirit and then as a body indicates the continuing physical presence of historical wounds, but it also emphasizes the body's role in identity and recognition. Beloved is clearly not content as a spirit; she requires her physical manifestation in order to be complete. As Sethe notes, "Paul D ran her off so she had no choice but to come back to me in the flesh" (200). Interestingly, Sethe's preoccupation is not with the spirit that lives in 124, but with Beloved's physical presence: "I only need to know one thing. How bad is the scar?" (184). It is the *body* of Beloved, not just the spirit—the spirit had been at 124 all along—which proves Beloved's presence and which comforts Sethe. Walking home from work one day, Sethe reflects that the smoke from the fireplace "was from a fire that warmed a body returned to her—just like it never went away, never needed a headstone. And the heart that beat inside it had not for a single moment stopped in her hands" (198). Sethe's observation exemplifies that it is Beloved's body, not her spirit, that proves her existence.

The novel therefore demands that the body be respected and reconnected to the spirit. As a spiritual healer who emphasizes reclamation of the body, Baby Suggs provides perhaps the best example in her sermon:

> [I]n this here place, we flesh; flesh that weeps, laughs; flesh that dances on bare feet in grass. Love it. Love it hard. Yonder they do not love your flesh. They despise it. They don't love your eyes; they'd just as soon pick em out. No more do they

love the skin on your back. Yonder they flay it. And O my people they do not love your hands. Those they only use, tie, bind, chop off and leave empty. Love your hands! Love them. Raise them up and kiss them. Touch others with them, pat them together, stroke them on your face 'cause they don't love that either. *You* got to love it, *you*! (88)

As the community's spiritual healer, Baby Suggs provides a powerful sermon that urges the fragmented people to love and reclaim their bodies. Regarding this scene, Yi-Lin Yu notes, "[W]hen Baby encourages her people to love their own different body parts that have long been neglected, forgotten, despised, violated, and destroyed, she exerts her maternal power to piece the broken fragmented selves of her people into a whole" (145). Similarly, Slattery notes that in this scene the "great epic wound of their ordeal as a people finds a salve that begins to heal their collective shame" (230). These readings are both accurate, but I argue further that Baby Suggs not only provides the means for communal healing by sharing collective wounds, but she also boldly contests the embedded Western philosophical separation of mind and body. Baby is considered a spiritual healer, yet she ironically encourages wholeness through the love and reclamation of the body. Therefore, Baby Suggs and her attention to loving the body provide a strong contrast to the Western concept of the body's inferiority and in fact show the body and the spirit to be inextricable entities.

The recognition of these shared bodily wounds and the reclamation of the body generate a strong sense of community; and ultimately, it is women's community that provides the means for healing in *Beloved*. The idea of communal healing in *Beloved* is not new, but it is important. For example, Carol E. Henderson's *Scarring the Black Body* points out the viability of community in healing collective wounds when she notes, "One comes away from Morrison's novel feeling that the scars of African American people run deep but, at the same time, that these wounds can be healed through a communal acknowledgment of their presence and a national recognition of their viability" (13). She notes later that Sethe's story is "the center of a communal healing that must acknowledge its *shared* historical legacy" (82). Likewise, Morgenstern notes that "*Beloved* stresses the importance of extra-familial community" (117). While these scholars emphasize healing through community, they fail to stress the significance of *women's* community. While a general community is vital, we recall Paul D's revulsion contrasted with Baby Suggs's and Amy Denver's acceptance, nurturance, and healing. Moreover, Sethe finds that she misses specifically the women's community she had acquired on arriving at 124: "[T]wenty-eight days of having women friends, a mother-in-law, and all her children together; of being part of a neighborhood; of, in fact, having neighbors at all to call her own—all that was long gone and would never come back" (173). Significantly, it is finally the return of that same women's community that forces the now-dangerous Beloved to leave. When thirty women, who act as what Patricia Hill Collins might call "othermothers"—women who communally assist each other by sharing maternal duties ("Meaning" 47)—come to 124, Beloved inexplicably disappears. The return of this female, communal support catalyzes the disappearance of Beloved.[11] As the physical incarnation of slavery's legacy, Beloved is a literal embodiment of the past, and she is driven out only when the community of women comes together to support Sethe.

While it seems paradoxical and troubling that a female character must be sacrificed to generate female healing, we remember that Beloved's reincarnation is not the original Beloved. Rather, she is a reminder of slavery's legacy, a growing physical manifestation of slavery's malevolence. Her reincarnation increasingly harms Sethe, so while Rushdy says that Beloved is "the embodiment of the past that must be remembered in order to be forgotten" ("Daughters" 571), I believe that she is also in fact a symbolic wound in need of healing. Her grotesque enlargement and infectious effects on Sethe and Paul D set her up as something injurious and painful. Yet the wound can be healed only with the community of women who have had similar experiences. It is Ella who recognizes and empathizes with Sethe's pain, for Ella herself had allowed her own infant (a product of her rape by "the lowest yet") to die (258-59). Hence, her leading role in the communal exorcism emerges from recognition, with Beloved symbolizing the shared wound. Since Beloved is the painful physical manifestation of many of their own histories, the women's communal response is what finally heals the wound, leaving only the scar of memory.

As Hélène Cixous reminds us, it is through female bonds that women can best find fulfillment, understanding, and healing (881). It is my claim that the relationships that comprise *Beloved*, as well as the following relationships in this study, are attempts to do just that—to create a communal recognition and healing between women by using the female body as a connecting point. The framework which is provided by *Beloved*, and which will be applied to some degree in each of the novels in this study, suggests that it is in community with others, particularly women who share in some of the memories, that historical fragmentations can be overcome.

Theresa Hak Kyung Cha's *Dictée*

A similar framework emerges in Cha's most successful novel, *Dictée*. As a child, Cha moved with her family to the United States from their homeland of Korea.   Cha's Korean heritage was consequently largely inflected by the Catholic education she received in the United States. Following her graduate education, Cha published *Dictée*, but sadly, during the same year the book was published, Cha was anonymously murdered in New York City.   Based on her early life in Korea—then occupied by Japan—followed by her family's immigration to the United States, Cha's literary themes understandably center on cultural displacement.   Even though *Dictée*, which is dedicated "To my mother to my father," is comprised of fragmentary biographical, autobiographical, and historical narratives, I identify the book as a novel due to its artistic and fictional elements and unifying themes.   As Stella Oh notes, *Dictée* does not fall easily into any genre, but rather, is a "compilation of multiple fragments of voices, images, and memories" reflecting "the haunting beauty and horror of that which had been forgotten and erased from the pages of [...] traditional history" (2). The novel centers on the experiences of displaced Koreans during the forcible and often violent Japanese occupation from 1910 to 1945.   Much like *Beloved*, Cha's disjointed, polyvocal style is reflective of the fragmentary history, culture, and geography of Cha's displaced ethnic group. More importantly, however, fragmented text is paired with images of fragmented bodies, a combination that serves to critique patriarchy, militarism, and the Western philosophical mind/body split.   Meanwhile, her depictions of mother/daughter relationships are her most poetic and significant relationships in this novel.   Therefore, this strongly resistant novel encourages empowerment through mother/daughter unity.

Literary Fragmentation in *Dictée*

Because the criticism on *Dictée* focuses so heavily upon its style and aesthetic, my comments on literary fragmentation will be brief.[12]   More important are the parallels between literary fragmentation, bodily fragmentation, and matrilineal bonds. *Dictée* critiques Western, patriarchal literary norms by making use of a postmodern, experimental style which reflects Cha's studies of the Modernists.   Including features such as disjointed narratives, large blank spaces, poetry, maps, diagrams, photographs, and large ideograms, all set within the framework of the nine Greek Muses, the novel creates a poignant statement on the fractured state of identity for Korean women and Korean Americans in the twentieth century. In contrast to the conventional novel form, *Dictée*'s multilayered and non-chronological style presents the voices of various women in various times and places. Because it allows for the voices of Koreans under Japanese occupation, Asian Americans, and women in general, Cha's powerfully feminist narrative style evokes Cixous's call to embrace "a *new insurgent* writing which [...] will allow her to carry out the indispensable ruptures and transformations in her history" (880). This new linguistic resistance will enable woman to liberate herself individually and will allow her to make a "shattering entry into history, which has always been based *on her suppression*," in Cixous's words (880). Hence, to write in a resistant and subversive way, or, as Cixous says, to "write in white ink" (881), allows woman to reclaim not only her writing, but also her speech, her body, and her history, and it is my belief that Cha's resistant and feminist narrative style does just that.

Dictée achieves this "new, insurgent" writing in various ways. For example, the prologue begins with an experimental paragraph that uses words and spaces in place of punctuation. The paragraph is written first in French and is then translated into English:

> Open paragraph   It was the first day   period   She had come from a far   period tonight at dinner   comma   the families would ask   comma   open quotation marks   How was the first day   interrogation mark   close quotation marks   at least to say the least of it possible   comma   the answer would be   open quotation marks   there is but one thing   period   There is someone   period   From a far period   close quotation marks   (1)

In this opening paragraph, Cha uses extra spaces to show where breaks in speech would occur if this paragraph were spoken aloud. This paragraph, with its rigorous attention to punctuation (and its ironic lack thereof) reveals the mechanisms of "standard English," suggesting the strict enforcement of an imposed language. Because this paragraph is followed by the narrator's exercises in the French language, the rituals of the Roman Catholic religion, and later the discussions of the strictly-enforced Japanese language in Korea, the novel presumably sets out immediately to critique imperialistic forces that impose behaviors and languages.

Another example of Cha's literary fragmentation occurs in the chapter "Erato/Love Poetry," a highly fragmented, feminist chapter filled with aesthetic rifts and gaps in text. Indeed, in some places, the reader must jump back and forth between pages to read coherently, and blank spaces indicate where the reader must do so. Sue J. Kim provides some insight, noting, "White space can be read generally as absence or silence, and has been associated more particularly with unwritten (or 'unshot') women's writing" (160). This idea of "shot" or "unshot" writing becomes especially relevant when a nameless woman enters a theater, presumably to see a film. Her every move is narrated as though she were on stage and these were her scripted stage directions. She is described as if she were being filmed:

> Extreme Close Up shot of her face. Medium Long shot of two out of the five white columns from the street. She enters from the left side, and camera begins to pan on movement as she enters between the two columns, the camera stop at the door and she enters. Medium Close Up shot of her left side as she purchases the ticket her full figure from head to foot [....] Long shot. Cut to Medium Close Up shot of her from the back. She turns her head sharply to her left. cut. (96)

Because the woman who is to be the spectator becomes the spectacle, the implication is that the female figure is, in Laura Mulvey's words, the "objectified other," the object of a "determining male gaze" (176). This controlling gaze is evident when Cha writes, "One expects her to be beautiful" (98). In other words, the chapter criticizes, via fragmented language and text, the objectification and fragmentation of the female body.

In another clear connection of fragmented narrative and social critiques—this time of patriarchy and militarism, the chapter "Melpomene/Tragedy" uses disjointed narrative to describe the splitting of Korea into North and South. Accordingly, this chapter is filled with fragmentary language that reflects rifts in language, speech, identity, history, and body. The chapter begins with a map of Korea, divided by a thick line. The subsequent language of the chapter includes lines such as, "Break. Break [....] Total severance of the seen. Incision" (79). Then, to clarify what this breakage means, when discussing her "Homeland," the narrator writes in a letter to her mother, "We are severed in Two by an abstract enemy an invisible enemy under the title of liberators who have conveniently named the severance, Civil War. Cold War. Stalemate" (81). The significance that the author of this letter attributes to the division is emphasized by the capital "T" she uses in the word "Two." Moreover, the division of the nation is described as something experienced bodily:

> I hear the break the single motion tearing the break left of me right of me the silence of the other direction advance before...They are breaking now, their sounds, not

new, you have heard them, so familiar to you now could you ever forget them not in your dreams, the consequences of the sound of the breaking. The air is made visible with smoke it grows spreads without control we are hidden inside the whiteness the greyness reduced to parts, reduced to separation [....] The stinging, it slices the air it enters thus I lose direction the sky is a haze running the streets emptied I fell no one saw me I walk [....] The streets covered with chipped brick and debris [....] Step among [rocks] the blood that will not erase with the rain on the pavement that was walked upon like the stones where they fell had fallen. (82)

The breaking of Korea is not only a political breakage. Rather, the split is experienced bodily, as something sensory that is felt, seen, and heard. Hence, the fragmenting of the homeland, or "motherland," is physically connected to the narrator's body, and the experience is shared with the narrator's mother.

Broken Bodies and Matrilineal Repairs in *Dictée*

The preceding examples of narrative fragmentation are closely paired with images of the female body, suggesting Cha's feminist call for women to reclaim the body. In fact, this call becomes immediately apparent in the novel's prologue, which describes the physical and psychological processes of speaking. The prologue depicts a diseuse, or female speaker, who Kun Jong Lee notes is probably "an immigrant girl" trying to speak like "native speakers" (82). Interestingly, the word "diseuse" denotes a woman who is skilled in speech and who performs monologues; in other words, this is a woman who is spotlighted as a sole speaker. However, in *Dictée*, the diseuse performs this role in great discomfort and under seemingly forced circumstances. The writing style includes italicized and non-italicized sections of narrative. The italicized portions ostensibly resemble the thoughts and psychological processes of the mind during speech, while the non-italicized sections narrate the physical process of speech. For example, the physical experience of the diseuse is a burdensome process:

The entire lower lip would lift upwards then sink back to its original place. She would then gather both lips and protrude them in a pout taking in the breath that might utter some thing [....] With a slight tilting of her head backwards, she would gather the strength in her shoulders and remain in this position. (3)

The description shows the physical movements and the discomfort involved in the diseuse's speaking. The subsequent italics, however, show the woman's internal thoughts, which are even more troubled: *"It murmurs inside. It murmurs. Inside is the pain of speech the pain to say. Larger still. Greater than is the pain not to say. To not say. Says nothing against the pain to speak"* (3). The italicized words point out the psychological trauma of being forced to speak, whether that forcing involves, in various places in the novel, the French classroom activities, the Catholic confession, or the imposed Japanese language. Further, the italicized sections seem to acknowledge a linguistic concession on the part of the woman. For example, *"She would take on their punctuation. She waits to service this. Theirs. Punctuation"* (4). Here, the speaker concedes to the dominant language. Therefore, mental and physical processes are interwoven; not only does the physical process seem torturous, but the psychological aspect of speech is even more tormenting, as this woman is forced into a language that she does not feel is hers. This section challenges the Western philosophical split between mind and body, showing how these processes are inextricable.

Moreover, the pairing of fragmented language and bodies indicates Cha's critique of the various forms of fragmentation that have characterized "women's historical condition" (Braidotti 121). *Dictée* includes at least three significant references to bodily fragmentation. As Vickroy points out, "characters' scars" often become "connecting points" (32). Similarly, I want to argue that these three images of wounding and scarring represent significant traumatic events, but that they are also shown to be points of connectivity between a daughter and mother, or, by extension, between women in general. As I argue in this section, the fragmentation of bodies in women's postmodern texts often emphasizes the possibility of combating historical fragmentation through women's bonds, and it also contests the patriarchal notion of the Western duality of body and mind.

In the midst of the "Diseuse" section is the appearance of the novel's first reference to bodily wounding, used as a metaphor for language: *"Inside is the pain of speech to say. Larger still. Greater than is the pain not to say. Says nothing against the pain to speak. It festers inside. The wound, liquid, dust. Must break. Must void"* (3). The narrator is stating that the difficulty of speaking a forced, foreign tongue is akin to bodily pain and wounding. Hence, the fragmentation of ethnic and racial identity resulting from the forced acquisition of language is parallel to the bodily fragmentation symbolized by the words "wound" and "break." The novel takes here a view that drastically differs from that of Western metaphysical dualities of body and mind. In this italicized section, which ostensibly refers to the diseuse's mental processes, Cha connects inextricably the functions of body and mind;

no longer separate, physical and psychological must function as one. As French phenomenologist Maurice Merleau-Ponty argues, the body is the condition through which a person experiences the world (29). The body cannot be, therefore, separate from the mind, for each is nonexistent without the other. Cha emphasizes this point in "Diseuse" by showing how internal and external processes are, in fact, inextricable from and dependent upon one another.

The wounds that come with the narrator's painful speech are given a solution later in the novel, when the narrator notes that the only safety from the "pain of speech" (3) comes from the mother's language: "Mother tongue is your refuge" (46). While "mother tongue" is another term for "native language," and hence does not necessarily imply a mother figure, the phrase is used here in conjunction with Cha's narrative of her own mother. Thus, the choice to use the term "mother tongue" is a conscious and symbolic one, connecting the mother figure with the idea of "refuge" or safety. The language of the mother, therefore, is a primary way of combating the pain and fragmentation experienced in the forced acquisition of language.

Moreover, in "Diseuse," the mother figure becomes a means of contesting religious patriarchy. In *Dictée*, Christianity—particularly Roman Catholicism—is viewed as a representative of Eurocentric, patriarchal hegemony. Just as the narrator is forced to speak the French language, she is forced to speak painfully her sins in the confessional. The Catholic Church is often criticized for its hierarchical power structure as well as its patriarchal rule. Accordingly, the chapter is filled with images of troubling linguistic and religious rituals with clearly gendered implications. The depiction of the Ash Wednesday Mass, for example, has been examined by Lee, who believes that the Mass "highlights the unbridgeable gap between a male priest and the female communicants in the Catholic ritual" (83). In these rituals, the male priest (not to mention God the Father and Christ the Son) is seen as the active catalyst for the Christian grace of the "women kneeling on the left side. The right side" (Cha 13), the recipients of the sacraments. These passive women are juxtaposed with the repetition of the masculine pronoun: "The Host Wafer (His Body. His Blood.) His [....] (Wine to Blood. Bread to Flesh.) His [....] To receive. Him [....] He the one who deciphers he the one who invokes in the Name. He the one who becomes He. Man-God" (13). Among the repetitious male pronouns, the lower-case "he" indicates the human male who becomes Godlike (with a capital "G") in his priestly capacity. The male incurs many powers in the Catholic Church, including the power to bestow God's forgiveness through penance and the all-important power to transubstantiate the bread and wine in communion.

However, this does not mean that the "Diseuse" section consigns women to a passive and powerless state. Rather, the section ends with a reference to the hope provided by the maternal figure of Mary, the "Holy Virgin" (18), the mother figure in whom many Catholic (and non-Catholic) women find empowerment. The chapter ends with the Novena, a prayer devoted to Mary: "NOVENA: NINE EACH. THE RECITATION OF PRAYER AND PRACTICING OF DEVOTIONS DURING A NINE DAY PERIOD" (19). The fact that this section, unlike the rest of the chapter (save the priest's questions on the preceding page), is entirely capitalized signifies its importance. Cha is evidently demanding the reader's attention on this final section of the chapter, which, following the helpless images of linguistic and religious patriarchies, boldly draws attention to the mother figure of the church. Immediately thereafter, the chapter's last line ends with a note of optimism, "And it begins" (19). The point of this first chapter may be to instill the idea that even within religions that have traditionally been patriarchal, there is hope provided by the mother figure; in other words, the hope attached to this initial mother figure suggests that women, too, can be saviors. Moreover, the Virgin Mary—the ultimate role model for Catholic women—sets the stage for other important mother figures in *Dictée*.

The second reference to bodily wounding occurs in the chapter "Clio/History," which tells the story of the young Korean revolutionary, Yu Guan Soon. This chapter, though dramatically fragmented, emphasizes unities, particularly those between women, families, and communities. A sixteen-year-old girl who leads the revolution against the Japanese occupation, Guan Soon is likened to the Christian martyr Joan of Arc as a historical foremother (28). Indeed, Guan Soon's body becomes the site of resistance when she is "stabbed in the chest, and subjected to questioning to which she reveals no names" (37). Guan Soon's corporeal wounding metaphorically represents the collective historical wounds of the Korean people during their colonization. In addition to Guan Soon's bodily wounding, history itself is described as fragmented via the metaphor of wounding:

> Why resurrect it all now. From the Past. History, the old wound. The past emotions all over again. To confess to relive the same folly. To name it now so as not to repeat history in oblivion. To extract each fragment by each fragment from the word from the image another word another image the reply that will not repeat history in oblivion. (33)

In this poetic segment, history is referred to as "the old wound," which, like a bodily wound, is reopened when the mistakes of the past are repeated. As Mas'ud Zavarzadeh and Donald Morton note, history is not a "closed narrative" (50), but rather, it must be understood as a "history of exclusions" (51). "History" is a system of ideas produced, maintained, and repeated by dominant forces, and it is used to perpetuate dominant ideologies (Zavarzadeh and Morton 16). And certainly, as Lee notes, this chapter "ultimately critiques the blindness of masculinist militarism and enlarges epic conventions to incorporate the experience of the vanquished" (88). Likewise, as Scott Swaner notes, "A recurring motive" in *Dictée* "is the desire to tell her stories in such a way that history will be frustrated, or more specifically, that history might not be repeated" (55). Cha agrees, pointing out that militaristic histories legitimate the dominant class by repeating destructive cycles and causing various fragmentations of body, identity, and history.

This chapter of *Dictée*, however, attempts to subvert these dominant patriarchal, racialized, militaristic ideologies by emphasizing unities within communities and families and between women. The chapter begins with a photograph of the revolutionary Guan Soon followed by, on the facing page, what seems to suggest a headstone inscription listing Guan Soon's dates of birth and death, along with a short epigraph, "She is born of one mother and one father" (25). We learn that family will play an important role in this chapter. In fact, the narrator conflates Guan Soon's family members by erasing punctuation between them: "The only daughter of four children she makes complete her life as others have made complete. Her mother her father her brothers" (31). The punctuation notably disappears between family members, indicating unity within the family.[13] Moreover, the first half of the passage indicates the "complete"ness that comes with either her familial unity or her role as a revolutionary. She has found wholeness where "others have made complete," either in her role of contesting dominant ideologies, or in uniting with her family members. Finally, the chapter ends with a photograph of three blindfolded Korean revolutionaries waiting, it seems, for their execution by the Japanese militia in the photo. This use of the revolutionaries' bodies visually promotes the significance of reclaiming the body and challenging patriarchal, militaristic, and colonial oppressions. Most importantly, the chapter immediately following, "Calliope/Epic Poetry," emphasizes reclamation of maternal bonds as a means of contesting patriarchal power. This chapter will be discussed separately following the final major reference to bodily fragmentation.

The third significant use of bodily fragmentation occurs in the subversive chapter "Urania/Astronomy," which uses poetic language and diagrams to emphasize bodily fragmentation. Rather than connect bodily wounding to history, as "Clio/History" does, this chapter's fragmented narrative again indicates the "pain of speech" (3), to borrow a phrase from the "Diseuse" section, as it examines this pain vis-à-vis the image of a woman giving blood. The chapter begins with an acupuncturist's diagram of the body's pressure points—a full, anterior and posterior view of the body—indicating that the body will become the locus for critique in this chapter. The narrator then describes the act of having a blood sample taken from her body, and she connects the process to a patriarchal view of woman's body: "One empty body waiting to contain. Conceived for a single purpose and for the purpose only. To contain. Made filled. Be full" (64). The syringe, created "for a single purpose," which is "to contain," becomes a metaphor for the patriarchal view that the female body is a vessel waiting to be filled, either sexually, by the male, or reproductively, by a pregnancy. This view, of course, is a biological essentialism which reduces woman to her reproductive capabilities. As Cixous asserts, a woman might desire a male body, but "not because she's deprived and needs to be filled out" (891). The image of drawing blood indicates Cha's similar criticism of this patriarchal perspective.

Meanwhile, we see another set of italicized words, similar to those of the "Diseuse" section, again symbolizing the psychological processes. However, this time, it is not the fear of speaking, as in "Diseuse," but rather, the experience of losing blood: "*Should it happen that the near-black liquid ink draws the line from point mark gravity follow (inevitably, suddenly) in one line down the arm on the table in one long spill, exhale of a spill*" (64-65). As in the "Diseuse" section, the italicized words are again juxtaposed with non-italicized words that explain the physical process: "It takes her seconds less to break the needle off its body in attempt to collect the loss directly from the wound" (64-65). Here, the wound is literal, unlike the metaphoric, historical wound in "Clio/History." This image of actual, physical bodily wounding continues the metaphor of drawing blood. However, this time, the action fails. Thus, the idea behind the feminized syringe, made for the "single purpose" of being filled, has, in fact, failed.

Following this section is another diagram, this time not of the whole body, like the chapter's first image, but rather, of the specific speech organs. The diagram shows the ways in which speech is directly connected to breathing and life itself. More importantly, however, is the comparison to be made between the chapter's opening diagram of the entire body, front and back, and the chapter's closing diagram of specific body parts. Eastern medicine traditionally views the body holistically, as shown in Cha's opening diagram, while Western medicine examines and treats specific parts, as the later diagram shows. Elisabeth A. Frost provides a key insight here, noting that "the concept of anatomy is foreign to classical Chinese medicine; the piecemeal approach to the body in Cha's later image reveals an emphasis on structure over process," and she continues, "There is no complete body imaged here; rather, the various diagrams represent a series of parts without reference to the whole" (188). Frost examines these images and explains the importance of understanding "*shen*," or "body/self," noting that, in Eastern medicine, "the entirety of inter-related parts, and the dynamic currents that transverse it, constitute *shen*, or body/self" (185). This idea reflects Rosi Braidotti's idea that contemporary medical technology (she refers specifically to reproductive technologies for women) serves to change "the body into a factory of detachable pieces" (61). In fact, the body and the mind are one and should therefore be treated as a whole, according to *Dictée*.

The three preceding examples of bodily fragmentation and their pairing with Cha's highly fragmented narrative strategies serve to critique colonialism, militarism, religion, patriarchy, and the fragmentation of the female body and identity. Fortunately, Cha, like the other authors I will discuss, provides a potential solution. By critiquing fragmentation of body and community, Cha suggests the safety that comes from connections with others. In particular, the best means of safety from the "pain of speaking" (a linguistic metaphor, as we have seen, for colonialism, militarism, and patriarchy), comes from the mother figure, for as Cha notes, "Mother tongue is your refuge" (46). Specifically, Cha praises mothers by dedicating an entire chapter to her own mother, portraying her as an epic hero in "Calliope/Epic Poetry." Like epic poetry, which begins with an invocation to the gods or muses, the narrator in *Dictée* apostrophizes, using the pronoun "you" to invoke her mother: "Mother, you are eighteen years old. You were born in Yong Jung, Manchuria" (45). Here, it appears that not only is the mother figure being invoked, but that Cha's mother has, in fact, become the chapter's (and perhaps the novel's) sole intended audience.

Then, Cha demonstrates maternal speech as a viable means for resistance to the patriarchal, colonial oppressions of women. As Trinh Minh-ha points out, gendered or racial "difference" from a dominant class (here, the Japanese colonizers, or perhaps, in *Dictée*'s broader context, the Euro-American/Christian/patriarchal/colonial/racist   class)   is   reduced   to "awkwardness or incompleteness. Aphasia" (80). In other words, difference from the dominant class becomes equivalent to the lack of speech. However, because Cha's mother continues to speak—and in fact teaches the Korean language that is forbidden—she finds a means of resistance: "The tongue that is forbidden is your own mother tongue. You speak in the dark. In the secret. The one that is yours. Your own. [....] Mother tongue is your refuge" (45). While "mother tongue" may mean simply "native tongue" or first language, the choice to use the word "mother" is deliberate and calculated. I believe that the use of the metaphor "mother tongue" here echoes Cixous; Cha and Cixous agree that women's voices and writing have been censored, and that patriarchal constraints have created a feeling of fear and guilt for women who want to express themselves, whether it is through their "mother tongue" or their writing. A further connection between Cha and Cixous comes when Cixous commands, "Write!" (876). Similarly, Cha says of her mother, "You write. You write you speak voices hidden masked" (48). It is unclear whether the statement is in the imperative, as is Cixous's, or whether it is a declarative statement. Regardless, the chapter reinforces the idea of the maternal, feminist language as a means of resistance.

As the chapter which focuses entirely on matrilineal bonds, "Calliope/Epic Poetry" includes perhaps the most significant and poignant passages of the novel, and it is based on the actual journals of Cha's mother, Hyung Soon Huo. The maternal presence as well as the need for women's writing and an insurgent female speech becomes particularly emphatic when the narrator describes her mother's visit to Cha's grandmother:

> You take the train home. Mother...you call her already, from the gate. Mother, you cannot wait. She leaves everything to greet you, she comes and takes you indoors and brings you food to eat. You are home now your mother your home. Mother inseparable from which is her identity, her presence. Longing to breathe the same air her hand no more a hand than instrument broken weathered no death takes them. No death will take them, Mother, I dream you just to be able to see you. Heaven falls nearer in sleep. Mother, my first sound. The first utter. The first concept. (49-50)

This passage is so moving, so matrilineal, so feminist, and so loaded that it will be examined at length. After the daughter is received by her mother, the narrator notes, "You are home now your mother your home" (49), and here, the importance of mother-daughter relationships becomes clear. Most significantly, the mother is equated with, and is inseparable from, being home. The passage connects this chapter to the novel's overarching themes of colonialism and diaspora by presenting a view of the "motherland" that is not only a homeland or a physical space, but is also a connection with one's mother. More interestingly, however, is the fact that punctuation disappears between "your mother" and "your home," blurring the boundaries; mother and home are, in other words, inextricable, and the implications here are enormous. First, the mother's body is the first "home" of every person. Second, this passage indicates that the presence of one's mother provides a safe space. Moreover, there is a unity here that is not present when Cha describes the fragmentation of speech, language, history, geography, and male-female relationships in other sections of the novel; unlike the other chapters, where fragmentation is unavoidable, this passage visibly blurs the comfort of home and the presence of the mother, a blurring symbolized by the absence of punctuation. In this woman-centered use of language, female bonds are not only implied, but they are also endorsed as a means of resistance to patriarchy.

The same passage continues, "Mother inseparable from which is her identity, her presence" (50). Here, the narrator notes that the maternal influence is, in fact, inextricable from one's identity; in other words, the mother figure in this novel is the determinant of identity. We might extend this argument to surmise that a disconnect from one's mother may, according to *Dictée* indicate a fracture in identity. The last lines of this passage indicate the significance and even the divinity of the mother: "Mother, I dream you just to be able to see you. Heaven falls nearer in sleep. Mother, my first sound. The first utter. The first concept" (50). Because "heaven" comes to her in sleep, the mother becomes divine or arguably Christ-like. Moreover, Cha reclaims the importance of matrilineage by pointing out again that motherhood is a child's first knowledge, a child's first word.

Dictée's praise of matrilineage continues when Cha extends the comparison of her mother and Christ. After a week of teaching her young Korean students, the mother falls ill. In her delusions, she is tempted by three women bearing appetizing plates of food. After each of the three temptations appear direct biblical lines from Christ's temptation by the devil following his forty days of fasting (see Matthew 4:1-4:11). Hence, the mother's temptation is likened to Jesus's temptation. We recall Cha's first chapter, in which she critiques Christianity while praising the Virgin Mary; here, Cha raises her mother to the status of Christ, clearly emphasizing the significance of mother-daughter bonds. The chapter pauses and interjects the Chinese characters for mother and father, and then it ends with a discussion of a fragmented body:

You leave you come back to the shell left empty all this time. To claim to reclaim, the space. Into the mouth the wound the entry is reverse and back each organ artery gland pace element, implanted, housed skin upon skin, membrane, vessel, waters, dams, ducts, canals, bridges.

Composition of the body, taking into consideration from conception, the soil, seed, amount of light and water necessary, the geneology (sic). (57-58)

We are reminded that it is with the mother that fragments become whole. Cha emphasizes this point by following this passage with another photograph of her mother. The larger implication is that it is through matrilineal bonds that women, particularly of racial and ethnic groups that are marginalized and oppressed, can understand the various fragmentations of identity, language, geography, and body that have been their "historical condition" (Braidotti 121).

Dictée ends, in "Polymnia/Sacred Poetry," with the story of a young girl and a young woman who meet at a well. The story, told from the perspective of the girl, praises the woman's generosity in sending a remedy for the girl's sick mother (169). Like the first chapter, which provides the Virgin Mary as a point of optimism and hope, this last chapter provides a final, hopeful image of sisterhood and healing. As the young girl comes home with the woman's remedy (And we are reminded that mother is equated with home), she sees in her house that "the shadow of a small candle was flickering" (170), a sign of hope for her mother's recovery, and perhaps a note of hope for all girls and mothers. The subsequent epilogue, then, comes from the perspective of another small child who begs her mother, "Lift me up mom to the window" (179). The vision the child receives from looking out the window provides a "picture image" that will "unleash the ropes tied to weights of stones" (179). While the child looks, "bells fall," with the implication that a church's bells are ringing (179). The mother's help has allowed the small girl to witness what must, to the women of *Dictée*, be a symbol of a patriarchal oppressor, for Cha has so rigorously critiqued the church in *Dictée*'s opening pages. But because the young girl feels this "image" will "unleash [...] the weights of stones," we are to assume, perhaps, that strength and vision provided by the mother can provide a start to resisting patriarchy.[14]

In both *Beloved* and *Dictée*, women authors of different ethnic backgrounds adopt disjointed writing styles with shifting viewpoints and timeframes, and they pair this literary fragmentation with images of fragmented bodies. This coupling becomes a political statement emphasizing the fragmented identity that occurs within the multiethnic communities of Morrison's African American and Cha's Korean heritage. Zavarzadeh and Morton's exploration of postmodernism shows it to be a means of political critique and resistance against dominant ideologies of racist and patriarchal oppression, and certainly, Morrison and Cha use their writing for these purposes. Moreover, they demand recognition between mothers, daughters, and communities. Appropriately, Cixous notes, "In women there is always more or less of the mother who makes everything all right, who nourishes, and who stands up against separation" (882). Certainly, both *Beloved* and *Dictée* encourage mother-daughter and communal bonds as primary ways to overcome women's historical position of fragmentation.

❈ CHAPTER THREE

Reliving African Matrilineage: Re-Membering the Past in Phyllis Alesia Perry's *Stigmata* and Gayl Jones's *Corregidora*

"For women of color, the subjective experience of mothering/motherhood is inextricably linked to the sociocultural concerns of racial ethnic communities—one does not exist without the other" (Collins, "Shifting" 58).

"Time's doorway remains open and Ayo and Grace have etched pain all over my body" (Perry 126).

When the first Africans were forcibly transported across the Middle Passage to the Americas in the early seventeenth century, a dichotomy between black and white was constructed. In the following centuries, people of African descent were continually seen by the dominant white Euro-American culture as inferior—undeserving of the most basic human rights. Even after "Emancipation" in the late nineteenth century, subsequent inequities were created by Jim Crow laws, "separate but equal" facilities, the rise of violent hate groups, and other forms of institutionalized racism. Now, in the twenty-first century, a guilty white American class has attempted to gloss over those violent historical events—to ignore the original American sin, to dodge any implication of guilt, and to deny the persistent effects. Therefore, in an effort to remember those events, to "rememory" the past, to borrow a term from Toni Morrison's Sethe, many contemporary black women authors have taken up the task of writing about slavery and its legacy. In these neo-slave narratives,[15] characters—often in contemporary settings—remember or even relive the events of the past. Among these writers are Phyllis Alesia Perry and Gayl Jones.

Perry's *Stigmata* (1999) and Jones's *Corregidora* (1975) portray the fragmented bodies of late-twentieth-century black women as vehicles for remembering (and re-membering) the past. Both writers use postmodern narrative fragmentation in order to shift back and forth in time. Similarly, both novels classify as what Tess Cosslett calls the "matrilineal narrative," which "either tells the stories of several generations of women at once, or which shows how the identity of a central character is crucially formed by her female ancestors" (7). Certainly, the protagonists are formed by their female forebears, and the novels also manage to tell the stories of several generations simultaneously. Moreover, according to Cosslett, these narratives have "a trajectory of misunderstanding, reconciliation, and final recognition between mothers and daughters" (8), recreating what Marjorie Pryse notes is the "tradition of female friendship and shared understanding" that "heals the lingering impact of separation imposed by slavery and sexism" (15). These observations anticipate my focus on mother-daughter recognition and healing in *Stigmata* and *Corregidora*, though I add that recognition and understanding are achieved through realization of bodily traumas. These two novels also effectively demonstrate the need for women to find creative ways of representing their matrilineal histories.

Unlike *Beloved*, which is "not a story to pass on" (275), *Stigmata* and *Corregidora* show familial legacies that refuse to be silenced. In *Stigmata*, Lizzie DuBose experiences the wounds of slavery as she relives her great-great-grandmother Ayo's enslavement in the nineteenth century. She also relives her grandmother's memories, which are intricately tied to Ayo's enslavement. Lizzie acquires literal wounds and scars to prove her connection to her foremothers' racialized past. On the other hand, in *Corregidora*, Ursa Corregidora relives the experiences of her great-grandmother, who was enslaved in a Brazilian brothel, and she struggles with the memory and physical scars of contemporary gendered and racialized oppressions. Both Lizzie and Ursa encounter wounding and scarring as a physical and metaphorical manifestation of their foremothers' presence.

Yet these women are not necessarily consigned to a life of pain and oppression. While Elizabeth Yukins suggests that Ursa's "historical trauma creates an insurmountable barrier to familial cohesion and inheritance" (222), I believe that Ursa and Lizzie resist this fragmentation. They discover that bonds with their mothers, grandmothers, great-grandmothers, and great-great grandmothers (ambivalent as these relationships may be) may help them to understand their histories and to begin healing. Moreover, they find new ways of being creative and remembering, such that they might end the painful cycle of their foremothers.

Carol E. Henderson's groundbreaking study, *Scarring the Black Body*, provides an excellent springboard for considering the historical contexts of the fragmented black body. Henderson points out that the scarring of the black body is unique in its historical context:

> The forced dispersement of Africans from their native land calcifies, for many, the indelible mark of cultural wounding prominent in the African and African American racial memory. The Middle Passage—that heinous voyage from Africa to the Americas in the belly of slave ships—lays bare the intricate mechanisms that facilitate not only the ruptures of a spiritual and cultural wholeness but also the formation of a linguistic system of suffering framed in the borderlands of the scar. (35)

Significantly, Henderson describes the initial displacement of Africans as the primary site of a collective cultural wound. Moreover, the physical and psychic wounds endured along the Middle Passage prove to be corporeal texts read later by buyers at the auction block:

> Thus the psychological and physical wounding of the black body in transit—in the watery space between the African and American coastlines—added an additional layer to the reading of, and a whole new dimension to the marking and scarring of, the black body in the context of America's chattel and bondage system [....] [T]he scar became a signifier for the rebellious African slave [....] Any scars found on a slave's body during this process [selling at the auction blocks] would let the potential buyer know the "temperament" of the slave—if the slave was a "problem" slave, one with a rebellious tendency. Amputated limbs, disfigured body parts, welted backs—all were read as manifestations of a rebellious spirit. Moreover, the slave's body served [...] as reminders to the black slave community of the consequences of rebellious action. (36)

In other words, the scar acts as a bodily signifier for the "type" of slave being purchased. The captive person's body and identity therefore become a commodity purchased with a sort of warning label.

But I argue that these scars are more than indicators to potential buyers; they are also the symbols of a shared heritage and a shared oppression for an entire group of people. The collective experience of whippings and mutilations during and after the Middle Passage becomes a means through which enslaved people could sympathize, unite, and rebel. I do not wish to suggest that there is any positive element whatsoever to these wounds and scars, but rather, that the memory of shared oppressions between enslaved or formerly enslaved persons forges a unity in spite of this most horrific of oppressions. For example, when *Beloved*'s Paul D kisses the scars on Sethe's back, the two share a moment of mutual healing (17). Henderson puts it well when she writes that the fragmentations of the enslaved black body "establish a cultural and literary genealogy that counteracts the commonplace callousness to black suffering, as the recognition of personal pain becomes an acknowledgment of communal pain" (38). Specifically, in *Stigmata* and *Corregidora*, scars also become a way for enslaved people to share and pass on stories, particularly through their matrilineage. As Sethe's mother tells Sethe of her branded scar in Toni Morrison's *Beloved*, "you can know me by this mark" (61). In retrieving, sharing, and reliving matrilineal experiences, women are brought into an experience to help both remember and heal the wounds of the past.

Phyllis Alesia Perry's *Stigmata*

Phyllis Alesia Perry was born in Atlanta and raised in Tuskegee, where *Stigmata* is largely set. After earning a degree in communications, she became a Pulitzer Prize-winning newspaper editor and journalist. Her first novel, *Stigmata*, is dedicated to "Arcola Johnson Perry and her sisters," Perry's mother and aunts, suggesting the value the author places on her own female forebears. For whatever reason, very little scholarship has been published on this deeply layered novel, leaving ample room for development around this important African American work.[16]

Stigmata tells the story of a young woman in Tuskegee, Lizzie DuBose, who literally relives, both physically and psychologically, the experiences of her foremothers. At fourteen years of age—the age, significantly, when her great-great-grandmother Ayo was taken from Africa (50)—Lizzie inherits a trunk containing a quilt and a diary. The items are passed to Lizzie from her grandmother Grace (who died in 1958, before Lizzie's birth in 1960). Grace instructs her sisters to bequeath the trunk to her granddaughter. Strangely, Grace's sisters, Mary Nell and Eva, instinctively know *"when the time is right and when it is she* [Grace's granddaughter] *will be waiting,"* as Grace's posthumously received letter to Mary Nell states (15). After opening this trunk, reading some of the diary, and exploring the stories on the quilt, Lizzie immediately begins to experience events from her grandmother's and great-great-grandmother's lives. Along with the psychic experiences, the wounds and scars that suddenly appear on her wrists, ankles, and back are those of her maternal grandmother and great-great-grandmother. Lizzie thus becomes the modern-day incarnation of slavery's legacy, inheriting the memories and the physical manifestations of slavery.

I describe Lizzie's experiences not as "reincarnation," but as "re-embodiment" because the women involved here are unique individuals with their own "varied and complex social reality," to borrow a phrase from bell hooks (*Feminist* 44). They do, however, share the physical manifestations of history. Thus, while she attempts to live her regular life, completing high school and enrolling in college courses, Lizzie's experiences become more frequent and more traumatic. By 1980, Lizzie's parents decide to institutionalize her, believing she is self-mutilating and suicidal. Then, for fourteen years, until 1994, Lizzie is institutionalized in several psychiatric hospitals. But to the perplexity of parents and doctors alike, Lizzie continues to be wounded by her frequent trips to the past. It is a priest who finally labels Lizzie's wounds as "stigmata" (213), which generally refer to the wounds of Christ. Father Tom rightly accepts that these wounds and scars are the literal manifestations of slavery, which connect Lizzie to her matrilineage as far back as her African American roots extend. Therefore, while she is the embodiment of slavery's legacy, she also finds that she has a goal; as the re-embodiment of her grandmother, she must make her mother believe in her experiences, thus bringing her mother into the circle of matrilineage. Lizzie must find creative ways of doing so, and her quest in a larger sense reminds African Americans to find ways of remembering their histories.

Gayl Jones's *Corregidora*

Like Perry, Jones is a southern writer whose hometown, Lexington, Kentucky, emerges in much of her writing. After earning her Ph.D., Jones became a professor at the University of Michigan, from which she mysteriously disappeared (Trudier Harris xii). She then published her second novel, *Eva's Man*, in addition to several plays and collections of poetry. Jones's influences include not only authors such as Alice Walker, Zora Neale Hurston, Carlos Fuentes, and Gabriel Garcia Marquez (Jones, "Gayl Jones" 283; Mills and Mitchell 3), but also blues singers such as Ma Rainey (Jones, "Gayl Jones" 285)—whose influences we see in Jones's bluesy, call-and-response narrative style. Her first novel, *Corregidora*, which she wrote in just three months ("Gayl Jones" 283), has been the subject of much scholarship,[17] but my analysis focuses on the connections between bodily wounding and scarring, the lived experience of matrilineage, and the necessity of claiming a matrilineal or women's community.

Jones opens *Corregidora* with the dedication "To my parents," and, as in the other novels in this study, the reader will come to understand the significance of mothers and fathers, whether compassionate, ambivalent, or tyrannical. Set in Kentucky in 1948 to 1969, the plot follows the journey of Ursa Corregidora, who is the female descendant, like Lizzie DuBose, of enslaved women. In this novel, it is Ursa's grandmother and great-grandmother who were enslaved by a Portuguese slaveholder and brothel-owner in nineteenth-century Brazil. As we learn, Ursa's great-grandmother and grandmother were forced to have sex with Simon Corregidora, who is therefore the incestuous father of multiple generations of Corregidora women. In fact, Ursa's mother and grandmother are offspring of Corregidora; in other words, Simon is both father and grandfather to Ursa's mother, and he is both grandfather and great-grandfather to Ursa. Like Lizzie and her foremothers in *Stigmata*, Ursa is compelled to carry on this horrific story. In fact, while Lizzie's main goal is to "reclaim" her "mother/daughter" (94), Ursa's main goal in life is given to her by her mother, grandmother, and great-grandmother, all of whom urge Ursa to "make generations" to bear witness to the tyranny of Simon Corregidora and the institution of slavery (10, 41, 101). This call to bear children in order to attest to Corregidora's abuse conflates the distinction Angela Davis makes between "breeder" and "mother," terms that Davis uses to explain the contradictory experience of black motherhood (7); Ursa's foremothers, however, see these roles as inextricable—to be a Corregidora woman in the past meant to be a breeder or a prostitute, and it now means giving birth to an extending Corregidora lineage, paradoxically keeping the slaveholder's name and legacy alive.

The rationale for "making generations" is given to Ursa when she is only five years old. Her great-grandmother tells her that the slaveholders "*didn't want to leave no evidence of what they done—so it couldn't be held against them*" (14). Therefore, Great Gram Corregidora says, "*I'm leaving evidence. And you got to leave evidence too. And your children got to leave evidence*" (14). This evidence must come in the form of offspring who can continue the oral tradition, because papers can be and have been burned: "*And when it come time to hold up the evidence, we got to have evidence to hold up. That's why they burned all the papers, so there wouldn't be no evidence to hold up against them*" (14). Presumably, the daughters they bear will stand as evidence to Simon's actions, though reproducing Simon's lineage is certainly a problematic way of bearing witness. It can be argued, then, that while the Corregidora women feel they are being resistant by transmitting their heritage to their daughters, they may also be perpetuating the role of the slave mother as breeder.[18]

However, while *Stigmata*'s Lizzie works toward her goal of reclaiming her mother, *Corregidora*'s Ursa becomes incapable, in the first two pages of the novel, of carrying on the Corregidora line. Ursa and her husband of four months, Mutt Thomas, have an argument on the back stairs of Happy's Café, where she sings for a living. Ursa falls violently, and while the scene is vague, I side with critics such as Madhu Dubey, Thomas Fahy, Katherine Boutry, and Janice Harris, who believe that Mutt pushes her down the stairs (Dubey 251, Fahy 213, Boutry 106, Harris 1), for, as Naomi Morgenstern argues, "Mutt is abusive all on his own" (110). Consequently, Ursa's uterus—which, we learn later, holds Ursa's one-month-old offspring (15)—must be removed. Ursa will not be able to bear her own daughter, and she thus effectively breaks her foremothers' cycle. Despite the fact that Ursa cannot physically carry on the lineage of Corregidora women, she finds other ways to carry on her foremothers' stories. In fact, like Lizzie DuBose, Ursa realizes that learning her mother's experiences is key to her own identity and self-understanding, and she finds a way to tell the story without bearing children. She also discovers that her bodily connection to her great-grandmother and grandmother reveals much about her own contemporary relationships with men. In other words, the body of Ursa, fragmented early in the novel, catalyzes the necessary retrieval of a personal and collective memory.

Narrative and Bodily Fragmentation in *Stigmata*

Both Jones and Perry have found that only a disjointed novel could successfully describe the experiences of Ursa and Lizzie as they re-"member" history. *Stigmata* is divided into two alternating strands of narrative, one narrating chronologically from June 1994 to July 1996 (the present-day period following Lizzie's release from the hospitals), and the other chronologically from April 1974 to March 1988 (the period when Lizzie begins experiencing her foremothers and is consequently institutionalized). While Lisa A. Long believes that this shifting narrative "deliberately unsettles reader expectations of plot linearity and causality" and "blurs the distinctions between normalcy and insanity" (134), I argue further that the alternating narration is necessary in order to exemplify textually the kinds of time shifts that Lizzie experiences. Her memory, after all, is a collection of nonlinear events, many of which she herself never actually lived. Moreover, the textual fragmentation also physically presents Ayo's insight from her diary: *"We are forever. Here at the bottom of heaven we live in the circle. We back and gone and back again"* (17). Lizzie learns this lesson as well, telling her mother, "Life [...] is nonlinear, Mother [....] The world seems to move in cycles, don't you think?" (93). Similarly, Lizzie's Aunt Eva (Grandmother Grace's sister) echoes this idea: "'Think of it like this,' she says calmly. 'The past—that's what you call it—is a circle. If you walk long enough, you catch up with yourself'" (117). This observation, like Ayo's and Lizzie's conceptions of circular time, is brilliantly presented in the fragmented narrative Perry creates, for the novel ends in 1988, just a few years before the novel begins in 1994. As Ayo, Aunt Eva, and Lizzie know, and as the reader finds out, we gradually come nearly full circle in Lizzie's life before the novel ends.

Coupled with this disjointed narrative, *Stigmata* also makes use of the fragmentary raced and gendered body in a way that exemplifies a collective historical wound. The black female body becomes the site on which the personal wounds of Lizzie's ancestors are inflicted. These wounds accumulate as Lizzie experiences not only her great-great-grandmother Ayo's enslavement, but also her grandmother Grace's (re)living of Ayo's experiences. Additionally, Lizzie experiences the pain Grace felt when she ran away from her family in an effort to escape Ayo's memories. Therefore, the reader might assume that, after her death in the future, Lizzie will have a granddaughter who will painfully experience all three women's lives. Any reader would find this prospect troubling: how could this cycle of pain possibly be an empowering phenomenon? It has been argued by Long that Lizzie is, in fact, experiencing a "rape" by her female ancestors, who forcefully take over her body and her memories. However, it is more likely that Lizzie will stop the cycle, choosing not to bear a daughter, for as Lizzie says, the circle eventually becomes complete (230), and thus, there is no reason to continue. Therefore, I agree with Stefanie Sievers, who more optimistically notes that the stories omitted from recorded history—even Lizzie's traumatic ones—must be engaged, for even though this experience can be "potentially isolating," it is also an "eventually rewarding endeavor" (131). Lizzie's experiences, as it will be shown, become rewarding endeavors because she reclaims her family's history, becomes creative in her own right through painting and quilting, and most importantly, reclaims her "mother/daughter" (94), Sarah.

The wounds and scars through which Lizzie accomplishes her goal take several forms. As Henderson points out, wounds and scars can be shown in "decay or disease, mutilation or fragmentation, or textualization in the shared experiences of a community" (114). Lizzie's wounds take several of these forms, and her suffering is, in Long's words, a "metonymic proof of a knowable past" (461), meaning that history is knowable in ways other than written historical records, which, as we know from *Corregidora*, can be destroyed. For Lizzie, history is transmitted in various ways: through her grandmother's written diary and narrative quilt, and by the actual psychological memories and physical experiences.

The novel opens in June of 1994, with Lizzie meeting Dr. Harper for the last time before she will finally escape the hospitals after fourteen years. She thinks, as she talks to Harper, of the "raised scars on my wrists" (2), and the "circles of raised flesh around my ankles" (5). In order to be released from the hospitals, Lizzie tells Harper that her claims over the last fourteen years—that she was experiencing the wounds of slavery—were "a rather elaborate delusion" (3). Lizzie now uses a "polished" story she has constructed to get out of the institution (3). She calmly says that she was twenty when she tried to commit suicide: "Having dreams about my long-dead relatives, that sort of thing. I had been having them for…let's see…since I was fourteen" (3); she states that she "used a paring knife" to hurt herself, for, "Confusion makes you do things like that" (5). This reconstructed history would seem to deny the stories of Grace, Ayo, and perhaps the entire African American community (whose experiences are effectively denied by the doctors). However, we discover that Lizzie has designs not only to leave the institution and again attempt a "normal" life, but also to share the experiences of her foremothers with her own mother.

As the novel progresses, we see Lizzie increasingly experiencing the wounds of her ancestors: "I have been moving in and out of mental landscapes with increasing frequency in the past two years, waking dreams constructed of strange vague memories. Often I find scratches and small raw scars on my body" (54). These inexplicable wounds and scars are a testimony to her foremothers' lives. As mentioned earlier, Henderson notes that scars during slave auctions "would let the potential buyer know the 'temperament' of the slave—if the slave was a 'problem' slave, one with a rebellious tendency," and moreover, those same scars became "reminders to the black slave community of the consequences of rebellious action" (36). Indeed, Ayo is one of those "rebellious" slaves, who attempts to jump overboard when she discovers that she is not going home to Africa (98). When she is pulled back aboard the ship, her wrists are mangled by the iron manacles, wounds that show up on Lizzie's body generations later. Then, the resistant Ayo kicks a white man at the market and is consequently hit "*cross the head with his hand*" (72). Ayo dictates these stories in 1899 to her daughter, Joy, who transcribes in the diary, "*One man there saw my arms and legs and the scars there and said something to the man what brung us off the boat Mama says.*" She continues, "*A man come and smear some bad smellin stuff on those raw sores on me. But it was a long time before they healed*" (109). As Joy writes, "*She pull back the sleeve of her dress and looks down at her arms for a long time. The marks are there, old but true*" (109). Ayo's body is marked with wounds and scars that suggest not only her traumatic history, but also her status as a slave and her potential for rebellion. In other words, the scars become part of her body and her identity, and they become revealing texts themselves.

Eventually, Ayo is whipped with such severity that her granddaughter Grace and her great-great-granddaughter Lizzie writhe in pain generations in the future when they relive the torture: "[*T*]*hat Ayo*," Grace tells Lizzie in the novel's central vision, "*she rushed in without warning and there I am flat on my back, wiping up blood from some old wound from some dead time*" (144). As Grace's spirit describes the experience to Lizzie, Lizzie sits up in her own bed in 1980 to "watch red drops seep through my skin, onto the quilt, onto the carpet" (145). She suddenly feels the severe pain of Ayo when she was whipped generations ago.[19] Because Ayo could not speak English until much later in her life, her new mistress, the seventeen-year-old, newly married Mrs. Ward, assumes Ayo is being disobedient:

> [Mrs. Ward] *comes back with two men. Big muscular hands. And Im scairt but Ida been even more if Ida known what she was up to. Shes carryin a whip and them two mens hold my arms while she whip me cross the back. Oh daughter she was laughin while she done it and them mens wouldn't look at me while I buck and try to get away. My dress fell away in big pieces and the blood ran down in the dirt and her pink dress was all splattered.* (172)

Showing the lived bodily legacy of slavery, over a century later, Lizzie's back is inexplicably and gruesomely mangled like Ayo's and subsequently Grace's. The violent whipping is what finally lands Lizzie in the first institution, and it explains why Grace left her family, for "*You can't sit still for that kind of thing. I had to go*" (145). Similarly, Lizzie now has to leave her own family to stay in the psychiatric institution. However, neither Lizzie nor Grace can escape the visions and wounds; like Ayo says of her own scars, "*They goes with me when I go to God*" (109).

In the institutions, however, none of Lizzie's numerous doctors understands what is happening to Lizzie. Instead, they rationalize the wounds by saying that Lizzie is depressed, suicidal, and self-mutilating. Certainly, none of the doctors believes that these wounds have been inflicted by Lizzie's dead foremothers, and they believe that Lizzie is simply delusional: "Every time I calmly explained to them [the doctors] that I knew reincarnation was real because Grace and I were living it, they said very pointedly, 'You're in denial, Elizabeth'" (70). The doctors' denial of any possibilities outside their own understanding of Western medicine may be indicative of a larger, systemic problem. Because of their immersion in Western philosophy, the doctors refuse to believe that Lizzie's memories could possibly become manifest on her body. Each of Lizzie's doctors knows of Lizzie's claim that a long-dead ancestor lived through such atrocities that her memories and wounds live on. Yet even though they cannot explain her "condition," they deny Lizzie's claim that she is the re-embodiment of Ayo and Grace, and they refuse to consider the option, given to Lizzie by a white priest, that she is experiencing a form of stigmata.

Their refusal may be indicative of a systemic white guilt and/or denial of the severity of slavery and its legacy. As James Baldwin argues in "The White Man's Guilt," "What [white Americans] see is an appallingly oppressive and bloody history, [...] a disastrous, continuing, present, condition which menaces them, and for which they bear an inescapable responsibility. But [...] they would rather not be reminded of it" (722). Thus, even though these doctors cannot explain the sudden appearance and abrupt healing of Lizzie's wounds, they stick to their story. Dr. Brun, for example, refuses to acknowledge Lizzie's explanation, even after Lizzie shows the doctor her scarred back and wrists:

> I turn them over so she [Dr. Brun] could see that each wrist has a perfectly circular scar, raised above the surface of the skin on my arms [....] Her gaze is hot, I can feel it as it steps tentatively through the maze of scars, from neck to waist and beyond, permanent remembrance of the power of time folded back upon itself. Proof of lives intersecting from past to present. (204)

Despite of her inability to explain Lizzie's state, Dr. Brun does not believe the story, nor do Lizzie's other baffled doctors:

A few days pass before Cremrick and the others notice that the scars have healed. They leave ugly marks that I will carry with me forever, but the grim wounds have closed over.

"Those scars look…" He looks at me probingly. "They look a few years old, I'd say. Now I know you were bleeding down there in the garden just a week ago. What is going on with you, Elizabeth?" (177)

This moment echoes the point that Gram and Great Gram Corregidora make—the dominant class maintains the ability to deny certain histories. Just as Simon Corregidora burns his paper records, the doctors' medical records present what the doctors want to maintain as the truth. Because the doctors refuse to comprehend Lizzie's explanation, Lizzie eventually—after fourteen years—fabricates a "realistic" story of attempted suicide, submits to their treatment, and is subsequently released.

The Fragmented Body in *Corregidora*

As in *Stigmata*, in Jones's *Corregidora*, the wounds of historical oppression become etched on the bodies of women, who must then find ways of healing. For the Corregidora women, the legacy of sexual slavery has wounded both the bodies and minds not of re-embodied, alternating generations of women, as in *Stigmata*, but of consecutive generations of women. Moreover, Ursa's fragmented body, which is deprived of its uterus in the first pages of the novel, signifies that Ursa must find other ways of healing since she is, at twenty-five years of age, unable to carry out her foremothers' command to "make generations" (10, 41, 101). This command is a problematic one which reifies the reproduction-as-commodity mentality of the slaveholder Simon Corregidora, but it is also a viable way for the Corregidora women literally to "bear" witness by reproducing daughters who will give voice to the women by carrying on the story. This mode of bearing witness through storytelling and reproduction stands in direct contrast to the means that slaveholders used—paper records which could be burned to hide evidence. The lineage of Corregidora women, however, comes to an end when Ursa has an emergency hysterectomy. The violence inflicted upon her body and her reproductive capability—which Ursa believes is integral to her and her foremothers' history—makes Ursa feel "as if something more than the womb had been taken out" (6). She laments that "part of my life's already marked out for me—the barren part'" (6). The fragmented body of

Ursa indicates a break in the historical legacy of Corregidora women, and Ursa must now forge a new way of connecting to and perpetuating her foremothers' legacy.

This initial reference to the fragmented body reinforces the body's importance as a site through which Ursa's foremothers' histories are invoked. After her surgery, Ursa moves in with Tadpole, the owner of Happy's Café. At one point, she notes, "When he was downstairs, I'd looked at the stitches across my belly again" (6). Her surreptitiousness of looking at the wound while Tadpole is away suggests the shame she feels about the loss of her womb. However, Ursa's note that she will "get back to work" as soon as the wound has healed indicates her determination to continue singing (6). In fact, she has found that without her womb, she is unable to give testimony in the same way as her foremothers. Therefore, she has decided to "give witness the only way I can" (54), and that is through singing.[20]

Interestingly, when the wound has nearly healed, Ursa is more open and even encouraging about the scar. She urges Tadpole to see it:

"The stitches are about gone," I said. He was still holding my arm. "You haven't seen the scar."

He said he hadn't looked.

"You can feel it," I said. "I can just reach down and feel it. It's going to leave a bad one." (17)

When Tadpole does not feel or look at the scar, Ursa "took his hand and put it under the sheet," asking if he "can feel it" (17). This scene shows Ursa's need for testimony, her need for someone else to understand her body's trauma. She significantly notes, "It's worse when you touch it than when you look at it," to which Tadpole replies, "I suppose. Most scars are" (18). This dialogue is significant on various levels. If we read this scar as a bodily representation of Ursa's patriarchal oppression vis-à-vis domestic violence, then we can understand how it is always worse to "touch it," or to experience it physically, than it is to witness, hear about, or read it. In other words, Ursa is, like her great-grandmother, grandmother, and mother before her, physically experiencing her oppression. And, like *Beloved*'s Paul D, Tadpole tries to sympathize with and care for Ursa 's wounds, but his refusal to look at or touch the scar recalls Paul D's sudden repulsion with Sethe's body. The suggestion is that, while Ursa needs someone to bear witness to her wounds, she will not find this witness in male company.

Ursa's scar can be read on several other levels as well, including the individual wounds of slavery, the metaphoric repercussions of generations of oppression, and the collective wounds of history. Bringing some of these ideas together, I read the scar as a reflection of both the bodily and psychological wounds that Ursa experiences through the Corregidora women's legacy. Like Laurie Vickroy, I believe that these scars, though representative of past oppressions, are also potential sites for connection (32). But I add to Vickroy's analysis that the wounds and scars are sites of *female* connection. Ursa recalls that her grandmother had told her to maintain the mental scars that represent women's imprisonment:

> *They burned all the documents, Ursa, but they didn't burn what they put in their minds. We got to burn out what they put in our minds, like you burn out a wound. Except we got to keep what we need to bear witness. That scar that's left to bear witness. We got to keep it as visible as our blood.* (72)

The use of the terms "wound" and "scar" are significant here. The wound refers to something that is meant to be gotten rid of: "you burn out a wound" (72). On the other hand, the scar is kept as a reminder of the wound, or in this case, as testimony to past experiences. In other words, the wound becomes a signifier of shared oppression, and while it is a symbol of oppression, it is also a way of bearing witness, uniting, and resisting.

Re-Membering Matrilineage in *Stigmata*

Ursa portrays the female body as a vehicle for connection between generations of women when she notes, "My veins are centuries meeting" (46). Similarly, Perry takes pains in *Stigmata* to make sure the women's connections are clear, that all the women are aware of the re-embodiment of Ayo, and that the "circle is complete" (230). While the men in the novel never know what is happening to Lizzie,[21] the women are eventually all connected in a web of female understanding. Ayo's return as Grace is accepted by Grace and her sisters, Mary Nell and Eva. Grace's return as Lizzie is understood by Lizzie, Aunts Mary Nell and Eva, and cousin Ruth. Only Lizzie's mother Sarah does not know, or perhaps refuses to understand, the reality behind Lizzie's experiences. Therefore, Sarah's understanding becomes Lizzie's primary goal in the novel. In fact, the failure of male characters and white characters to comprehend Lizzie's situation sets up a gendered and racialized dichotomy in which the African American woman—

facing such multiplied forms of hostility and discrimination that Zora Neale Hurston calls her "de mule uh de world" (14)—must unite with her foremothers and female relatives in order to reclaim their history. Lizzie realizes that she must reclaim Sarah as her mother/daughter, and she must find a creative way of doing so.

Of course, the relationship with foremothers is anything but pleasant. In both *Stigmata* and *Corregidora*, the foremothers generate extremely painful experiences for their descendants. However, these painful experiences offer ways of knowing and remembering that make the protagonists' histories relevant in the twentieth century. As I mention in previous chapters, I do not claim that matrilineal histories and women's bonds are without conflict. Rather, they are often full of pain and ambivalence. But it is in the physical experience that the protagonists are able to remember (and re-"member") their familial histories. The foremothers are reminding their female descendants not to let their history die, painful as it may be. Significantly, it is through the wounded and scarred body that these women are all connected, and the wounds and scars serve as reminders and connecting points for all the women of the novel. As Lizzie says of herself, her grandmother, and her great-great-grandmother, "We stand there together in her battered body, bent doubled with pain" (123). Although they share a body, we recall that each woman's struggle is unique and personal, rejecting, as bell hooks rejects, the idea of a "common oppression" (*Feminist* 44). *Stigmata* emphasizes this distinction by limning out the differences between Grace and Ayo in Lizzie's memory. For example, while both women are anxious for Lizzie to remember their stories, "Ayo paces back and forth inside my head. Restless and yearning, impatient for me to remember all. But Grace holds our secrets just beyond my view, eagerly teases me with imminent revelations" (165-66). In other words, the women have clearly distinctive personalities, between which Lizzie can distinguish. Despite their differences, both women use Lizzie's body as a text for re-membering their stories. As Lizzie poignantly says, "Time's doorway remains open and Ayo and Grace have etched pain all over my body" (126).

The woman who initiates the process of re-embodiment and scarring is Ayo, an African woman who was, at age fourteen, captured and brought to the United States, where she was enslaved under the name Bessie Ward. Ayo's story is reborn in her granddaughter, Grace, and Grace's story is reborn in her granddaughter, Lizzie. This is not the actual rebirth of Ayo and Grace; rather, it is the recrudescence of their memories, manifested physically in their granddaughters. It is as though Joy's and Sarah's bodies are the vehicle for Ayo's and Grace's memories to emerge in subsequent generations. We know Ayo's story as it is dictated to her daughter, Joy, and recorded in Joy's diary. From Ayo's words, it is clear that having her story remembered is her primary concern. Hence, she passes her story and her name to her daughter: "*My name mean happiness she say. Joy. That why I name you that so I dont forget who I am what I mean to this world*" (7). Ayo then explains that her people's history must be remembered, and she also indicates that her lineage will not be stopped:

> *I come from a long line of forever people. We are forever. Here at the bottom of heaven we live in the circle. We back and gone and back again.*

> *I am Ayo. I remember.*

> *This is for those whose bones lay sleepin in the heart of mother ocean for those who tomorrows I never knew who groaned and died in that dark damp aside a me. You rite this daughter for me and for them.* (7)

When Ayo says she and her people want to be remembered, she suggests that she will continue their memory however she can. The pronoun "This," which has no clear antecedent, may mean that something Ayo is doing is meant to honor those Africans who have died along the Middle Passage. However, the later repetition of these final lines, the first lines Lizzie reads from the journal (though they now have some slight, unexplained alterations), emphasizes Ayo's intention to perpetuate her story in some way:

> *We are forever. Here at the bottom of heaven we live in the circle. We back and gone and back again.*

> *I am Ayo. Joy. I choose to remember.*

> *This is for those whose bones lie in the heart of mother ocean for those who tomorrows I never knew who groaned and died in the dark beside me. You rite this daughter for me and for them.* (17)

We notice the addition of the word "choose" in this second version, showing that Ayo actively carries on this memory. More interestingly, the word "rite" offers several interpretations. At first glance, it appears to be a misspelling of "write," for Joy is writing the dictated diary for Ayo and presumably for the people who died along the Middle Passage. However, Ayo may have also intended the word "right," meaning that she wanted the sin of slavery to be "righted" or corrected. If we read it in this light, we understand why Ayo may have come back to haunt her descendants. Their memory, Ayo believes, will allow the horrible story to be carried on and perhaps, somehow, rectified.

Appropriately, while Ayo is dictating these lines, Joy notes that Ayo is sewing a baby quilt. Then, on her deathbed, Ayo indicates that she knows that Joy will have a baby girl: *"Take care of that little girl she say"* (231). After Ayo's death in 1900, Joy becomes pregnant with her first child, Grace. Because this passage occurs at the end of the novel, we know that the baby girl is, in fact, the memory of Ayo being reborn. Grace, of course, does not learn her role until she begins reliving her grandmother Ayo's experiences. And although Joy deeply misses her mother—*"it was like somebody knocking the breath out of my chest"* (230)—when Joy discovers she is pregnant, she takes some comfort: *"I miss her, but it aint so bad now that this child jumps for joy in my body"* (231). The word "joy," of course, is significant here, and we know that Ayo's spirit is rejoicing to have found a way to perpetuate her story.

Grace, born in 1900, then relives the horrific experiences of her grandmother, her body becoming the site on which her grandmother's historical wounds are revisited. Much like Lizzie will do almost half a century later, Grace attempts to live a regular life, though her days are often torturous and painful, and she finds herself bleeding from her wrists and ankles. She marries George, and they live in the small cabin that Ayo and her husband bought after their "emancipation" (a term that is used loosely here). Grace has three children—twins Frank and Phillip, and daughter Sarah. However, by 1940, Grace can no longer tolerate the experiences of Ayo, which at times literally floor her: *"[T]hat Ayo, she rushed in without warning and there I am flat on my back, wiping up blood from some old wound from some dead time"* (144). On the night when Grace relives Ayo's whipping, she determines that she must leave Johnson Creek. She believes she can escape the memories and thus avoid institutionalization, which in this era would have been a "bona fide asylum" (158).

By 1945, Grace seems to have come to an understanding of Ayo's plan to have her memory reborn in her female lineage, for she composes a letter to her sister, Mary Nell. In this letter, she says that she, too, will pass her story on, but that the memories will not be reborn in her daughter: *"I could not curse her* [Sarah] *with these things that are happening to me* [....] *I know I can't pass it on to her this craziness. So save it but not for Sarah. Maybe Sarah will be safe"* (15). Grace then hints that her story will be perpetuated in her not-yet-conceived granddaughter:

I feel that others after us will need to know. Our grands maybe will need to get these things. Please leave these for my granddaughter. I know she aint here yet. But I have faith that you and Eva will know when the time is right and when it is she will be waiting. (15)

Grace does not pass the story onto her daughter in order to ensure that her memories will be reborn *by* her daughter. Grace dies in 1958, and two years later, in 1960, Lizzie, Grace's only granddaughter, is born. Therefore, Mary Nell and Eva know that these items must be bequeathed to her. Some ambiguity arises with why Mary Nell and Eva decide to wait until Lizzie's fourteenth birthday (the age at which Ayo was taken from Africa), but as we will see, Lizzie's aunts seem to be part of—or at least to understand—the re-embodiment process.

Grace discovers that one way of carrying on the story is through a quilt that portrays Ayo's experiences. When she receives it, interestingly, Lizzie calls this quilt a "cloth womb," saying that she is "tangled" in it, but that "it feels good" (39). This feminized quilt, in other words, encourages Lizzie's painful but necessary reconnection with her foremothers. During one memory in 1980, for example, Lizzie glimpses a photograph of Grace while she begins to doze on her mother's sofa. Suddenly, she finds herself sitting at a mirror, looking at a face that is "both familiar and strange," both her own face and that of her grandmother (52). Lizzie has become Grace, a fact which is proven when Sarah, now a tiny child, calls, "Mama!" and runs into the room: "'Sarah, baby, slow down!' I hear the words come out of my mouth, and I gasp. [...T]he child, a girl of four or five, stumbles and trips [....] 'Brought your basket, Mama...' she says, biting her little lip" (53). As she speaks to Sarah, Lizzie thinks, "Or is it Grace saying it? I don't know. I'm so well-cocooned inside her past that words flow from me automatically" (54). The symbol of the mirror represents the foremothers' insistence on a cross-generational reflection of their memories. In other words, when Lizzie looks at her grandmother, she also looks at herself. The face of a foremother in the mirror indicates that the women, though individuals, are "cocooned" or interconnected with the stories of their own mothers. Importantly, it is not the quilt that causes the memories; rather, Lizzie learns these stories partly through Joy's diary, partly through the quilt's visual stories, and primarily through the actual reliving of the experiences (a point which is proven by the fact that Lizzie knows many stories and details that are *not* included in the diary and quilt). The quilt and diary are, according to Aunt Eva, "just the keys that unlock the door to what you call the past" (118). The quilt comes to represent metonymically Ayo's and Grace's histories, "keep[ing] visible" the past, to borrow a phrase from Ursa Corregidora's grandmother (72). Just as bearing witness is considered a "scar" to Ursa's foremothers, the quilt becomes a metaphor for the body in that it visibly testifies to the experiences of Lizzie's foremothers.

Eventually, Lizzie understands that she is actually reliving the experiences of Grace. And because Grace had experienced the life of Ayo, Lizzie's experiences inextricably reflect both these women:

> Ayo—Bessie—has invaded Grace's memories and she can't keep things straight in her head. Ayo is there, reminding us who we are. And we can't stop the sea from rolling beneath us and we can't stop the fear. The chains go on over our skin, no matter how much we holler. We don't understand what the white ones say and they don't understand us, but they know they are hurting us, don't they? (57)

Again, while the women's memories are inextricable from one another, the women themselves remain separate entities with distinguishable personalities. Lizzie notes that Grace's experiences are more vivid because of the accumulation of physical and psychological wounds: "Grace always speaks loudly, her memories hissing insistently inside my head. And behind her are the dream-like tangles of Ayo's life. More distant but also more painful" (87-88). The women have unique experiences, but these experiences are tied up in one another, combining into one unbearable collective memory.

The night when Grace decides she must leave her family is one of the most significant scenes in the novel, for all three women are together in one body. The scene so clearly represents the idea of collective memory, both physical and psychological, that I quote it at length:

> I look down at Grace's hands. I smooth those over Grace's dress, feeling awkward in the longish skirt, missing my jeans. This is a little different and odd. There is no merging, just an awareness of Grace, off to the side, doing the same things, sensing the same things I do. She moves closer. I keep looking over my shoulder, almost expecting to find her standing there with me. But she nudges me from the inside and I try to resist, to listen to her without becoming her.
>
> *But you're already here,* she whispers. *This is your own self talking to you. Don't you understand? Ayo and me, we're here.*
>
> A spasm of pain sears my back. I gasp, trying to keep my focus, and in that moment Grace steps forward and takes the blow. We stand there together in her battered body, bent doubled with pain [....]

Grace is restless. She's been fighting inside with memory. Ayo has been ever
present, and Grace goes through the day crumpling under the weight of the old
African's pain. (123)

In this scene, all three women, though distinct entities, struggle within the
same body. This scene clearly demonstrates the ambivalent relationship that
many women throughout this study have with other women. While it
appears that Grace is purposefully inflicting pain upon Lizzie, it is also Grace
who tries to soothe the pain. As Lizzie finds herself being whipped, Grace
"steps forward and takes the blow," effectively sharing and easing the
wounds that Lizzie is receiving.

Unfortunately, these experiences are unheeded by Lizzie's parents.
Lizzie eventually accepts that "Bessie [Ayo's American name] became
Grace, and Grace became me. Me, Lizzie" (47), and she finds that there is
no real separation in the women's experiences: "Grace is with me—or I am
with her" (56). Or, more simply put, "I was Grace" (73). But like the
doctors, Lizzie's mother and father refuse to believe that Lizzie is actually
experiencing Grace's and Ayo's lives. Interestingly, Lizzie does not concern
herself with her father's understanding; instead, she focuses her efforts on
helping her mother to comprehend. The reason that her mother's
understanding is more significant is perhaps because Lizzie recognizes that
"[e]very woman needs her mother" (153), but more importantly, because
Sarah is, in fact, her daughter.

Lizzie begins to feel guilt for having abandoned her children as Grace,
though she also realizes that she had little choice. Why she does not concern
herself with her twin boys, Sarah's brothers, is because "I feel as though
Sarah and I had the tighter connection. You know? Mother-daughter-
mother" (222). Sarah was a very young girl when her mother left the family,
and the abandonment seems to have affected Sarah more deeply than it has
her brothers. The twin boys are ten years older than Sarah, and because they
were nearing adulthood and had the close companionship of each other, they
were ostensibly better able to accept their mother's disappearance.
Furthermore, Lizzie/Grace now has the deeper connection with Sarah in her
new life as Sarah's daughter. As Lizzie puts it, Sarah "could pretend that her
mother was merely an unpleasant memory, someone she could die mourning,
though I was right here waiting to embrace her as my child" (70). In other
words, it is just as important for Lizzie's real experiences to be understood as
it is for Grace to repair the rift caused by her abandonment. While Ayo's
motive is to remember the people lost along the Middle Passage, Grace's
motive is to reclaim her abandoned daughter. These objectives can both be

accomplished through Lizzie, who must now find creative ways of remembering Ayo's story and reclaiming Sarah as both mother and daughter.

To do so, Lizzie determines to make her own quilt that will portray Grace's story in addition to the intersections between Ayo's, Grace's, and Lizzie's lives. She decides on the quilt because Grace's quilt so thoroughly represents Ayo's and Grace's stories; therefore, she rightly believes that another quilt will help Sarah to see and accept the re-embodiment of her own mother. Lizzie determines that the "edge of my new quilt needs blood red" since "[b]lood binds three lives" (61). As the "mother-daughter-mother" (222) pair begins the quilt, Sarah is surprised and confused to find that Lizzie knows how to do appliqué skillfully; initially, Lizzie lies and says she took a course on appliqué at the institution in Birmingham. But in reality, Lizzie learned from her memories of Grace, and she now wishes to teach Sarah, just as Grace would have done. When she insists Sarah work on the quilt with her, Sarah asks, "Are you sure you want me to help you with it?" Lizzie responds, "Oh, yes. I'm not going to do it without you" (67). She requires her mother's help so that Sarah will witness the reconstruction of history.

At first, the quilting endeavor seems fruitless. As Lizzie notes, "The pictures I've designed for that quilt so obviously tell Grace's story that I'm beginning to think Mother is deliberately pretending to be the densest woman on the planet" (169). The relationship that forms while the two women quilt, however, resembles an inverted mother-daughter relationship, with Lizzie as the mother and Sarah as the daughter (reminiscent of the inverted mother-daughter relationship that occurs between Sethe and Beloved, though without the malevolence). While quilting, Lizzie acts as an instructor, teaching her mother/daughter how to do appliqué. As Sarah learns, Lizzie feels the pride of a mother: "I've shown Mother how to quilt, [...] and I watch with what can only be described as growing pride at her enthusiasm" (194). Meanwhile, Lizzie subtly tries to explain her life to her mother: "'Life,' I say, "is nonlinear, Mother.'" Sarah responds, "Depends on how you look at it. You may see it as a circle. But it always seems like a line to me [....] The past is past." Lizzie replies, "Well, I like circles [...] The world seems to move in cycles, don't you think?" (93). In this frustrating exchange, Lizzie seems about to burst: "I want to stand up and declare myself to her, cry, 'I am the circle! The circle stands before you!'" (94). Lizzie "feel[s] as if I've come back from death and exile just for the moment when the light of recognition glows from her eyes" (95). She disappointedly thinks, "Maybe she'll never be able to open the door to the possibility that I could have been right about being Grace. About being Ayo" (70). Yet they continue the quilt together, and Lizzie maintains hope that her mother will soon be drawn into her history.

When Lizzie breaks the news to her parents that she will be leaving Tuskegee when the quilt is finished, her parents are shocked. Sarah, in particular, looks at her with "child's eyes," and Lizzie feels guilt, because "I did this to her. First as her mother, then as her daughter" (196). When Sarah says, "'I don't know if I can let you go again," Lizzie responds, "Yes you can, Sarah," and she notes that her mother "doesn't blink when I say her first name" (198). And just as Lizzie had hoped, as the quilt nears completion, Sarah finally begins to accept the validity of Lizzie's claim. Lizzie comes behind Sarah one day in the attic, with the quilt spread in front of her "like a gushing wound": "Lizzie. You know this woman. You got the story…from her" (225). Lizzie responds, "Sarah," and then "wonder[s] if she's noticed that I call her by her first name" (226). As Sarah gradually and reluctantly accepts the truth of the re-embodiment, Lizzie thinks, "The circle is complete and my daughter sits across from me with the gap finally closed" (230). The novel provides closure with Lizzie accomplishing her main goal, which is to reconnect with Sarah, her "mother/daughter" (94).

Interestingly, characters who do not experience their foremothers' lives often sympathize and even empathize with characters who do. Grace's sisters, Mary Nell and Eva, fully understand Grace's experiences. Moreover, they understand and even anticipate Lizzie's experiences. More interesting, Lizzie's cousin Ruth, granddaughter of Mary Nell, actually witnesses Lizzie's reliving of Grace's and Ayo's lives. This connection displays the novel's insistence on women's bonds, for Ruth is "the closest thing to a sister I have" (36), and although Ruth is not directly implicated in these experiences, she becomes a participant in them. In 1980, just by touching Lizzie around her wrists, Ruth can experience the past: "'Lemme see.' She holds out her hands and I give her mine. Turning them over, she examines the wrists [....] She puts her hands around my wrists and lets out a small gasp, dropping them as if they are hot" (83). She says she feels "[p]ain" and that "[t]here's more coming. Coming fast" (83). Ruth understands immediately, asking, "How is it that you can step into the life of a woman who died before you were born?" (84). That night, Ruth becomes part of Lizzie's vision, a "dark girl in African clothes" who pulls Lizzie onto the bridge over which Lizzie has jumped, seeing it, in her vision, as the rail of a slave ship (84-88). And even at the moment when Lizzie doubts Ruth's sisterly understanding (when Ruth finally visits Lizzie at the hospital after two years), Ruth can still empathize:

She turns my hands over, sliding her fingers over the scars on my wrists. At first it's an examination, then a communication between us. A spasm of pain crosses her face, then it's calm again.

"I'm sorry they hurt you," she whispers, with a secretive, painful smile. She's crying a little. "I don't know why they have to do that." (193)

While Ruth always senses Lizzie's pain, she also knows that Lizzie's mother will have trouble accepting the truth. Ruth believes that Sarah "knows," but that she "doesn't wanna believe" (75). Even Ruth, who avoids Lizzie for two years, is part of the web of female understanding, proving how powerful the female historical connections have become.

Finally, Mary Nell and Eva's understanding shows the fullness of women's connection in this novel. The feminist understanding, as shown with Ruth, includes both matrilineal and sisterly ties. When Mary Nell receives Grace's letter in 1945, she inexplicably knows that she must give Grace's trunk to a not-yet-born granddaughter. It appears that Mary Nell and Eva have accepted and perhaps, like Ruth, even participated in some of Grace's experiences. For both aunts know, without hesitation, that the trunk must be given to Lizzie on her fourteenth birthday. In 1980, before Lizzie's institutionalization, she visits Aunt Eva at Johnson Creek, and Eva indicates that "Mary and me understood 'bout these things, but…everybody else woulda called [Grace] haunted or something, you know. It woulda scairt George outta his pants. No tellin' what he woulda done. We couldn't let it get out" (117). As they talk, Eva suddenly calls Lizzie "Grace," and she tells Lizzie/Grace that she should not run away from her husband and children. While Lizzie is, at the moment, experiencing another scene from the past, the scene raises the question of whether Eva knows what Grace/Lizzie was/is going through. As Lizzie listens to her aunt/sister speak, she realizes that "this seventy-something woman is my sister. And my granddaughter" (118).

The novel does not note any further conversations between Eva and Lizzie until Lizzie's Christmas visit in 1986; when Lizzie, to her mother's horror, uses a curse word, Eva laughs and says under her breath, "Still making trouble I see, Gracie" (218). Lizzie notes this instance, reflecting in her hospital journal later, "I found myself strangely comforted by Aunt Eva; she called me by her sister's name and for the first time I had confirmation that Eva did understand, she knew who I was" (218). The next instance of Eva's understanding comes in July 1994, when she says to Lizzie regarding Sarah, "Take it slow […] Someday she'll understand better" (49). And indeed, Sarah is the only woman who is not aware, or chooses to be unaware, of Lizzie's re-embodiment. Fortunately, Sarah, like all the other women of this matrilineage, eventually comes to understand, ensuring that "[t]he circle is complete" and that "the gap finally closed" (230). Sarah's absorption into this larger web of female understanding demonstrates the novel's overarching call for women's bonds as an effective means of remembering history.

As Long points out, "An experiential bodily connection to slavery has been lost. No one alive bears the physical scars of African American enslavement" (459). Yet Perry experiments with just what would happen if that were, in fact, the case—if descendants of enslaved persons could indeed experience their ancestors' pasts to the degree that these experiences are physically manifested on their bodies. But Perry is doing more than portraying the bodies of female descendants as sites on which the wounds of history are etched. Perry is also doing more than using the body as a vehicle for remembering the past. She is using this marked body as a means of reclaiming the African American family that has been affected in so many ways, and of ensuring the survival of black women's histories. As Lizzie knows, "I'm supposed to be reclaiming my family" (29), and particularly, "reclaiming my sixty-one-year-old daughter" (93). It is important to recall that, for Grace, the goal is to heal the rupture with her daughter caused by her abandonment, while for Ayo, the objective is to remember those lost in slavery. Lizzie's body tells the story of both her grandmother and great-great-grandmother, and most of the women in the novel fully comprehend Lizzie's bodily experiences. As Lizzie believes, "Every woman needs her mother" (153). In order for Lizzie to feel complete, she must reclaim her own mother/daughter, whose burden it is to accept that Lizzie is both mother and daughter. Because both women occupy the position of "mother/daughter" to the other, the novel effectively conflates matrilineal generations such that the relationships themselves and the bodies they are harbored within are unified. In the end, healing comes from Lizzie's and thus Grace's reconnection with her mother/daughter.

Reclaiming Women's Bonds in *Corregidora*

As in *Stigmata*, the women of *Corregidora* are connected inextricably through their collective memories. The process of remembering in *Corregidora*, however, is strikingly similar to Toni Morrison's conception of "rememory," which Sethe explains in *Beloved*: "If a house burns down, it's gone, but the place—the picture of it—stays, and not just in my rememory, but out there, in the world" (36). (Likewise, even if Simon Corregidora burns his paper records, the essence of his actions is still alive.) This type of memory is distinguished from what happens to Lizzie DuBose in that Lizzie's memories inflict real and tangible marks on her body. Ursa's memory, on the other hand, comes from the physical and oral tradition that her great-grandmother, grandmother, and mother perpetuate. Their repetition of stories creates a cycle of existence for the Corregidora women whereby their experiences are indelibly etched in the memories of each new generation. But similar to Lizzie's memories, the stories told by Ursa's female progenitors become inextricable from the memories of each woman, such that the memories of the previous generations become part of Ursa's memory. When Ursa's mother shares her story with Ursa, "[S]he wasn't Mama now, she was Great Gram talking" (124). As Mama says of her own mother and grandmother, "They just go on like that, and then get in to talking about the importance of passing things like that down. I've heard that so much it's like I've learned it off by heart" (128). But as Ursa notes, it seems that "she had *more* than learned it off by heart, though. It was as if their memory, the memory of all the Corregidora women, was her memory too, as strong with her as her own private memory, or almost as strong" (129). And interestingly, there is a connection beyond the retelling of stories whereby Ursa takes her foremothers' memories as her own. Her mother says to her, "I know about those other things you would never let me know," a confession which tells Ursa, "She was telling me she knew about my own private memory" (122). In other words, the memories of the Corregidora women operate not simply in a top-down mode, and in fact, the memories of the younger generations perhaps reflect back to the older generations, too. The stories told by Great Gram and Gram Corregidora not only serve to perpetuate their stories, which they want remembered. These stories also serve to create a cyclical existence for the Corregidora women, who incorporate the memories so thoroughly into their own minds that they relive the bodily and psychic experiences in their own contemporary ways. Specifically, the women re-create the corporeal experiences of Great Gram Corregidora, viewing their bodies as vehicles for perpetuating their lineage and giving voice to the women's experiences.

When Ursa is only five years old, her great-grandmother tells her the story of "Old man Corregidora": "the Portuguese slave breeder and whoremonger [who] fucked his own whores and fathered his own breed" (9). These women, raped and forced into prostitution, "did the fucking and had to bring him the money they made. My grandmamma was his daughter, but he was fucking her too" (9). As Ursa recalls, Simon Corregidora "*took her* [Great Gram] *out of the field when she was still a child and put her to work in his whorehouse while she was a child*" (10). Great Gram "*was the pretty little one with the almond eyes and coffee-bean skin, his favorite*" (10). As exemplified in this brutally incestuous scene, Corregidora clearly sees Great Gram as a sexual commodity, calling her a "*good little piece. My best. Dorita. Little gold piece*" (10). Ursa recalls the storytelling:

> Great Gram sat in the rocker. I was on her lap. She told the same story over and over again [....] It was as if the words were helping her, as if the words repeated again and again could be a substitute for memory, were somehow more than the memory. (11)

The telling, therefore, becomes the means of historical memory, and Great Gram clearly expects Ursa to tell the story to her own daughter someday. Great Gram tells her devastating story of rape and prostitution in her own words:

> I remember the day he took me out of the field. They had coffee there. Some places they had cane and then others cotton and tobacco like up here. Other places they had your mens working down in mines. He would take me hisself first and said he was breaking me in. Then he started bringing other men and they would give me money and I had to give it over to him. (11)

Great Gram notes that she stole a picture of Corregidora, which is now in Ursa's possession, because "*afterward when evil come I wanted something to point to and say, 'That's what evil look like'*" (12). When Ursa asks if Great Gram is telling the truth, Great Gram angrily slaps her:

> When I'm telling you something don't you ever ask if I'm lying. Because they didn't want to leave no evidence of what they done—so it couldn't be held against them. And I'm leaving evidence. And you got to leave evidence too. And your children got to leave evidence. And when it come time to hold up the evidence, we got to have evidence to hold up. That's why they burned all the papers, so there wouldn't be no evidence to hold up against them. (14)

The slap is reminiscent of when Sethe's mother slaps her in *Beloved*, a punishment that comes with Sethe's request to have a brand similar to her mother's (61). In *Beloved*, however, a young girl is slapped by her mother for desiring the physical manifestation of her status as a commodity, while in *Corregidora*, a young girl is punished for questioning that status. In other words, the women telling the stories expect those stories to be understood, heeded, and carried on—not repeated, as a young Sethe seems to desire, or misrepresented, as Great Gram Corregidora fears. Clearly, it is Great Gram's intention to raise generations of women who will bear witness to this history of enslavement and sexual oppression.

Ursa's grandmother, who is both daughter and "mistress" to Corregidora, also tells the story of Corregidora's horrific tyranny. It was during Gram's infancy that slavery was abolished. Yet Gram shows the legacy of remembrance that characterizes this family: *"Naw, I don't remember when slavery was abolished, cause I was just being born then. Mama do, and sometime it seem like I do too"* (79). Gram also acknowledges that her duty is to "bear witness" when she states that, after Emancipation, *"the officials burned all the papers cause they wanted to play like what had happened before never did happen. But I know it happened, I bear witness that it happened"* (79). Gram notes that although the women enslaved in the brothel were now free, most of them had been *"put down in the rut so deep, that that's bout all they could do now"* (79). Great Gram, too, stayed at the brothel after slavery *"until,"* Gram notes, *"she did something that made him wont to kill her, and then she run off and had to leave me"* (79). We find out only at the end of the novel, when Ursa discovers what this *"something"* is, what exactly has happened between Great Gram and Corregidora. After Great Gram flees, Corregidora begins having sex with Gram; surprisingly, Great Gram does not return for her daughter until 1906, when Gram is eighteen and pregnant with Ursa's mother.

While Great Gram and Gram's experiences are very similar, after Emancipation, these experiences are not possible for Ursa's mother, who is born not on the Brazilian plantation or in Corregidora's brothel, but in Louisiana. However, Ursa's mother finds herself in a relationship that closely echoes the relationships Great Gram and Gram had with Corregidora. But unlike Great Gram's and Gram's stories, Mama's story is not retold, but rather, silenced. Ursa wonders about her own father and why Mama does not share her story as Gram and Great Gram do. As Ursa notes, "I couldn't be satisfied until I had seen Mama, talked to her, until I had discovered her private memory" (104). Retrieving Mama's story becomes Ursa's main goal in the novel, as her mother's story is the one she is lacking in her collective memory: "[S]*he wouldn't give me her own terrible* [memories....] *I never saw her with a man because she wouldn't give them anything else*" (101).

During her visit with her mother in Bracktown, Mama finally tells Ursa her story. She had met Martin, Ursa's father, at a restaurant, and as Mama describes her relationship with Martin, she did not feel love, nor did she have a desire to stay with him. Rather, she realized that she only wanted a daughter, noting that it was "[l]ike my body or something knew what it wanted even if it didn't want no man. Cause I knew I wasn't lookin for none. But it was like it knew it wanted you. It was like my whole body knew it wanted you, and knew it would have you, and knew you'd be a girl" (114). Like her foremothers, Mama has internalized the view that a daughter must carry on the story. However, Mama remains silent on her story. Unlike Great Gram and Gram, Mama seems to feel some level of guilt for having perpetuated this history, for having brought Ursa into the cycle. At one point, Mama notes, "*You carry more than his name, Ursa*," and Ursa "*knew she had more than her memories. Something behind her eyes. A knowing, a feeling of her own*" (103). In other words, Mama somehow understands what Ursa is going through and seems to feel responsible. This guilt may be one reason why Mama does not tell and retell her story as do her foremothers. It may also explain why Gram had enjoyed Ursa's singing; she may have seen it as a new way to remember, while Great Gram did not like it, perhaps because it threatened her own way of bearing witness. Clearly, the Corregidora women are complex and unique individuals, and Ursa's mother seems to silence her own story in order to protect Ursa from yet another troubling history.

Mama, like her mother and grandmother before her, had wanted a man only for reproductive purposes. She initially accepts Simon Corregidora's view of the body as a commodity, though she subversively views this reproductive capacity as a way of giving voice and memory to the wounds of the past. She views the Corregidora women's bodies, in other words, as sites on which historical wounds are etched, but also, paradoxically, as the means through which shared wounds may be given testimony. As Mama says to Ursa, "They'd tell me, they'd be telling me about making generations, but I wasn't out looking for no man" (112). Scholars have made the point that Mama and her foremothers use men for reproductive purposes.[22] Therefore, what I add is the connection of bodily fragmentation to the need for matrilineal bonds in order to generate understanding between generations. This need for matrilineal bonds is echoed in the layered parallel between this novel and *Stigmata*, both of which exemplify an overarching need for women's connection. When Mama says, "I knew you was gonna come out a girl even while you was in me. Put my hand on my belly, and knew you was gonna be one of us [....] I knew my body would have a girl" (117), she parallels Perry's *Stigmata*, in which Ayo knows Joy will have a baby girl

(230), and Grace knows Sarah will have a baby girl (15); these women know, in other words, that their bodies will be the means of literally "bearing" witness to their historical wounds by bearing girls to carry on the story.

However, not only do the Corregidora women continue the tradition of wanting a baby girl without the father, a "parthenogenetic fantasy" to borrow Morgenstern's phrase (106), but they also perpetuate the ambivalent and frustrated relationship that Great Gram had with Simon Corregidora (173). As Cheryl Wall points out, the women perhaps unwittingly "have imposed the role of stud on the men with whom they 'make generations'" (117). Martin's frustration with the Corregidora women emerges when he sees Gram powdering her breasts; he stares at her because, as Mama says, "he wasn't getting it from me" (130). Mama uses Martin as a vehicle for her own daughter, and otherwise, she refuses him her love and sexuality: "I hadn't even given myself time to feel anything else before I pushed him out [....] Just that one time" (118). She becomes pregnant due to "that one time," and afterwards, she does not visit him. Gram goes to Martin to persuade him to marry Mama, but even then, Mama refuses his sexual advances. Finally, a frustrated Martin leaves the house where Mama, Gram, and Great Gram live. Two years later, when Mama visits him, he brutally beats her and tears her clothes, sending her into the street, "lookin like a whore" (121). His volatile response is explained by Harris, who notes that the Corregidora "family history refuses to recognize love" (2). Indeed, the inability of the Corregidora women to express love or passion towards men becomes a source of deep agitation for the men, including Martin, Mutt, and Tadpole. (Of course, Martin's violence should not be excused.) Martin's anger is eerily prescient of Mutt's violent frustration with Ursa. Moreover, this relationship echoes and drastically complicates the relationship between Great Gram and Corregidora. Mama says of Martin, "I carried him to the point where he ended up hating me, Ursa. And that's what I knew I'd keep doing. That's what I knew I'd do with any man" (121). A generation later, Ursa proves that Mama's suspicion may have been true. For both Mutt and Tadpole end up hating Ursa, though Mutt eventually proves what Great Gram discovered long ago about Simon Corregidora—that he "can't get her out of his mind" (184). The tyranny of Simon, perhaps, urges the Corregidora women to see men merely as vehicles for carrying on the Corregidora legacy. Thus, while Great Gram elicits ambivalence from Simon through a sexual act, Mama and Ursa gradually turn love into hate with Martin, Mutt, and Tadpole by failing to reciprocate the men's feelings.

What is interesting is the repetition of the ways in which women are oppressed; after Emancipation, these women are still seen as sexual objects. This repeated oppression is evidenced in the language that men and women use. For example, when Ursa uses profanity, Mutt asks, "How'd you get to talk like that?" Ursa responds, "I guess you taught me. Corregidora taught Great Gram to talk the way she did" (153). What Mutt does not realize is that his own language also echoes the language Corregidora had used when talking to Great Gram. For example, Mutt says, "Your pussy's a little gold piece, ain't it, Urs? My little gold piece" (60). This language reflects Great Gram's note that "I was his little gold pussy, his little gold piece" (124). The men unwittingly shore up a system that continues to oppress all African Americans, but which doubly oppresses black women as sexual commodities.

The Corregidora women also relive the sexual experiences of Great Gram and Corregidora. In Simon Corregidora's brothel, he reserves Great Gram, "his little gold piece," for himself (124). He insists on approving men before they may have sex with her, and he will not allow men who are "too black" (124). He would, however, send "white mens" to her, telling the white men "he had tested me out hisself" (127). This scenario, in which the Corregidora women are viewed solely as sexual commodities, is repeated in several subsequent generations. Gram's story is a nearly exact replica of Great Gram's story, as she, too, is enslaved in this brothel (even after Emancipation) and is reserved as Simon Corregidora's personal whore. But one mystery shrouds the relationship between Great Gram and Corregidora. Decades ago, Great Gram discovered a sexual act "*that make him hate her so bad he wont to kill her one minute and keep thinking about her and can't get her out of his mind the next*" (173). This one element of their sexual relationship is kept quiet—"*Up till today she won't tell me what it was she did*" 172)—and it is Ursa who, a century later, discovers what "it" was. Ursa completes the cycle when she discovers this maneuver, repeating Gram's words in her mind, "What is it a woman can do to a man that make him hate her so bad he wont to kill her one minute and keep thinking about her and can't get her out of his mind the next?" (184). In this "moment of pleasure and excruciating pain at the same time, a moment of broken skin but not sexlessness," Ursa sees the cycle in its completion:

It was like I didn't know how much was me and Mutt and how much was Great Gram and Corregidora—like Mama when she had started talking like Great Gram. But was what Corregidora had done to *her*, to *them*, any worse than what Mutt had done to me, than what we had done to each other, than what Mama had done to

Daddy, or what he had done to her in return, making her walk down the street like a whore? (184)

In 1969, at age forty-seven, Ursa discovers the painful sexual act that Great Gram had performed on Corregidora such that she had obtained some amount of power. Ultimately, it is the recognition of this unknown element of Great Gram's history that helps Ursa feel healed. As troubling as this ending is, Ursa does discover some completeness by unearthing this element of her great-grandmother's history. Although the ending is ambiguous, I believe that when Ursa discovers her great-grandmother's subversive sexual act and uses it on Mutt, the reader is to assume that Ursa, through remembrance and repetition of her great-grandmother's corporeal act, has regained some element of empowerment in solidarity with her foremothers and in resistance to patriarchy. Moreover, as Boutry correctly argues, Ursa uses this act of "orality toward reconciliation" (115). Unlike the other novels in this study, *Corregidora* presents the potential for a workable heterosexual relationship. When Mutt says, "I don't want a kind of woman that hurt you," and Ursa eventually responds, "I don't want a kind of man that'll hurt me neither" as she "fell against him crying" (185), it is clear that Ursa has found a new way to relate to Mutt. She has found a way to be creative through singing her stories, she has learned her mother's story, and she has finally shown, by crying, the possibility of emotional connection. In each of these senses, Ursa has moved in a direction that may make a healthy relationship possible.

We recall that the repetition of her foremothers' lives stops when Ursa becomes unable to make her own generations. When Tadpole asks Ursa, "What do you want?" Ursa responds, "What all us Corregidora women want. Have been taught to want. To make generations" (22). However, Ursa's thinking finally expands to consider whether bearing new generations is the best way, or whether this is merely Corregidora's patriarchal thinking:

> But I *am* different now, I was thinking. I have everything they had, except the generations. I can't make generations. And even if I still had my womb, even if the first baby *had* come—what would I have done then? Would I have kept it up? Would I have been like *her*, or *them*? (60)

Building from her own mother's ostensible guilt, Ursa begins to question the logic of her foremothers' tradition, even though she disagrees with Tadpole when he points out, "Procreation. That could also be a slave-breeder's way of thinking" (22). As Morgenstern notes, "The past repeats itself in the novel not only because it is traumatic, but also because forms of power endure"

(110). In other words, even after Emancipation, the Corregidora women continue to be traumatized and brutalized by a racist, patriarchal hegemony. Ursa's loss of her womb, however, encourages her to find other ways of remembering her foremothers' stories without using her body as a vessel. Like Lizzie DuBose, who discovers quilting as a means of creative remembering, Ursa uses her singing to tell her stories. Moreover, as Morgenstern argues, "In *Corregidora*, maternal telling has the force of literalization, a force which undermines representability. The past is not simply transmissible from generation to generation; it repeats itself" (108). Therefore, like *Stigmata*'s Lizzie, who states that "the circle is complete" when her mother knows the full story, *Corregidora*'s Ursa completes the cycle by learning her mother's story and Great Gram's secret. When Ursa gets on the bus to leave Bracktown after hearing her mother's story, "suddenly it was like I was remembering something out of a long past" (132). Ursa's way of healing involves the discovery of her own creative individuality as well as the recognition of her foremothers' hidden stories. In knowing her mother's story, Ursa feels a sense of fulfillment in better understanding her own history, which she ostensibly will carry on through her talent for singing.

In the end, both Lizzie and Ursa are stronger than their foremothers, a strength represented in at least three ways. First, of course, they have each repaired the fractures in their matrilineage—Lizzie by reclaiming her mother/daughter and Ursa by connecting to her mother and remembering her great-grandmother's actions. Second, they both gain individuality. While Ursa and Mutt come together in the end, Ursa is now interested in him as more than just a father for her offspring. She takes a position of power and then begins to cry—both elements of Ursa that we have not seen, and she effectively separates from her foremothers' tradition. Lizzie moves to Atlanta in spite of Anthony Paul's clear disappointment, and she is able now to separate from her parents, on whom she has been largely dependent. Finally, Ursa and Lizzie have both found creative new ways of remembering and sharing their foremothers' histories. Lizzie finds a way of remembering through her painting while at the hospitals and through quilting when she comes home. Similarly, Ursa has moved beyond "making generations" and is now creative in her own right as a singer. Thus, Lizzie and Ursa remember and reclaim their matrilineage while finding new ways of creating memories, and while doing so, they effectively reclaim their own identities.

❈ CHAPTER FOUR

Childhood Scars and Women's Love in Emma Pérez's *Gulf Dreams* and Paula Gunn Allen's *The Woman Who Owned the Shadows*

"With phrases I create you. I create you here in text. You don't exist. I never wanted you to exist. I only wanted to invent you like this, in fragments through text where the memory of you inhabits those who read this" (Pérez 138-139).

"Text: my body—shot through with streams of song" (Cixous 882).

The previous chapters serve as examples of the healing powers of feminist bonds. But what happens if those bonds are not accepted by society? As I have mentioned throughout this study, I do not wish to argue in favor of a "traditional" family unit—a heterosexual, heteronormative, father-mother-children unit that serves to re-cycle its own power structures by generating children who are themselves products and perpetuators of the hetero-familial structure. Nor, however, do I wish to argue against it. Rather, I want to suggest that an unconscious or noncritical assimilation into *any* established ideological structure concretizes hegemonies that re-create themselves. If entered into conscientiously, the family unit can provide a stable and compassionate environment. However, if entered into by familial or social pressure or compulsion—even if this compulsion is unconscious or internalized—this structure can serve to promote a patriarchal, heteronormative, and racist regime. In this chapter, Emma Pérez's Chicana novel *Gulf Dreams* (1996) and Native American author and theorist Paula Gunn Allen's *The Woman Who Owned the Shadows* (1983) will demonstrate the ways in which the hetero-familial unit is reinforced and recycled; on the other hand, they will also show how the conscientious subversion of this structure can provide a potential site of resistance against dominant patriarchal, racialized, heteronormative regimes of power.

Specifically, "childhood scars" (Pérez 98) connect the protagonists to their lovers in both novels: The nameless narrator and the young woman from El Pueblo remember their fifteenth summer when they fell in love, and Ephanie and Elena separate as children when their families discover their blossoming romance. Ephanie's central conflict is the struggle for identity when she learns that she was complete only in the presence of her female childhood friend and adolescent lover. Significantly, Ephanie seems to struggle towards a "conventional" family life, though clearly this is not what she wants. She has been socialized to accept this structure as the norm even though she desires the companionship of Elena, a Chicana girl from a neighboring village. Similarly, Pérez's protagonist is pressured by society and threatened by men—particularly her lover's husband Pelón—to pursue a "traditional" heterosexual union. Paradoxically, it is because these women are prohibited from uniting that Pérez's and Allen's works subversively emphasize sisterhood and female sexuality as means of a racialized woman's survival and resistance to patriarchal, racist, and heterosexist oppression.

After earning her doctorate degree in history from U.C.L.A., Chicana author Pérez began publishing critical and theoretical work on multiethnic, feminist, and queer theories. Her first novel, *Gulf Dreams*, has not been the subject of much scholarship, even though it is one of the first Chicana lesbian novels ever published.[23] Award-winning author, critic, and theorist, Allen was the daughter of multiethnic parents—a Laguna Pueblo, Sioux, Scottish mother and a Lebanese father. She was raised in New Mexico between reservations, and spent most of her childhood education at a convent school. These elements of her childhood recur throughout her writing, particularly in her semi-autobiographical *The Woman Who Owned the Shadows*. After earning a graduate degree in creative writing, Allen began to explore the woman-centered, Laguna Pueblo stories her mother had shared with her. Allen is best known for her essays and poetry, yet scholars have largely ignored *The Woman Who Owned the Shadows*.[24] This chapter, therefore, provides a necessary examination of bodily and narrative fragmentation, as well as women's unity as a form of healing.

Both Pérez and Allen masterfully employ postmodern narrative to explore the experiences of their female protagonists. As Barbara Smith paraphrases Bertha Harris, "[I]f in a woman writer's work a sentence refuses to do what it is supposed to do, if there are strong images of women and if there is a refusal to be linear, the result is innately lesbian literature" (qtd. in Smith 11). While several of the novels in this study might be examined in this light, *Gulf Dreams* and *The Woman Who Owned the Shadows* provide some of the most nonlinear plots we have yet examined. Pérez's narrative fragmentation involves a nonlinear series of vignettes, dreams, and memories, and while the novel follows a traditional three-part structure, formed by the sections "Confession," "The Trial," and "Desire," it carefully subverts the conventional novel genre. The visual and spatial fragmentation of the novel creates the impression of breaks in time and purposeful lapses of memory. For example, surrounded by large white spaces is the sentence, "I would not see her again for a year" (18), a visual indicator of the loss the narrator feels. The novel also includes the key postmodern element of self-referentiality, as *Gulf Dreams* refers to the constructed nature of the novel itself and addresses the audience. For example, the narrator notes, "I thought writing this years later would release me from her. But I feel no reprieve" (27). Again, at the end of the novel, the narrator refers to the novel as a creation: "This part of the story has to be over, even though I don't believe in endings. I believe in the imagination, its pleasure indelible, transgressive, a dream" (157). Here, the narrator emphasizes her break with the Western ideal of narrative objectivity. Since the European Enlightenment, the ideal of objectivity pervades literature; this passage, conversely, indicates that a novel is a subjective text, and in this semi-autobiographical novel, the author/narrator is, in fact, a subject showing how heteronormativity has fragmented her life. Hence, only a fragmentary, subjective style could adequately portray the narrator's experiences.

Similarly, Allen's novel, *The Woman Who Owned the Shadows*, portrays Ephanie, a Guadalupe Indian, experiencing the fragmentation of Native American history and of contemporary heteronormative life. Ephanie struggles against what Allen, in *Song of the Turtle*, calls the "victim" role of second wave Indian fiction (9), surviving, but also resisting the labels of the victimized and "noble" Indian espoused by Teresa's white, liberal friends (*Woman* 140). As Ephanie herself learns more about her heritage and her own connection to the legendary woman who fell from the sky, the reader experiences the interconnections of white American and Native American cultures. Therefore, the novel is fragmented with Ephanie's contemporary story and traditional Native American cultural stories. The narrative exemplifies Ephanie's cultural fragmentation specifically when it negotiates between contrasting spiritualities of European Christianity and Native

American culture: "Bless me, father for I have sinned," a Christian confessional invocation, is contrasted on the same page with, "Bless me, Naiya Iyatiku, for I have been wronged" (153). Ephanie struggles to identify herself both as an "American" and as an Indian, but she finds that the split identity is impossible. Her name itself is described as "a split name, a name half of this and half of that: Epiphany. Effie. An almost name. An almost event" (3).   This name, however, is "proper for her, a halfblood.   A halfbreed," or a fragmented being (3).   In sum, both novels use narrative fragmentation—in the visual text, the chronology, the story, and the characters' identities—to show the elusiveness of wholeness presented to women of minority ethnic, racial, and sexual identities.   These authors employ the fragmented body, which, as Judith Butler notes, is not a passive, "mute facticity," that is written upon (*Gender Trouble* 129), but which is, rather, an active agent in the interpretation and performance of history. Indeed, the bodies of these women become agents for memory, texts which represent the trauma of their inability to love.[25] Thus, both novels display the completeness that can come with loving relationships between girls and women

Heteronormativity in *Gulf Dreams*

Pérez's *Gulf Dreams* is set in contemporary, small-town, rural Texas, the place which Gloria Anzaldúa calls the "borderlands."   At this juncture of racial, ethnic, cultural, and religious differences, identity is often difficult to pinpoint.   Appropriately, the novel contains a number of wounded and scarred bodies, representative of fragmented identities.   The narrator says early on that her body prevents her from fitting into her own family, for she has "[h]air and eyes so light that I could pass through doors that shut out my sisters and brother.   Their color and brown eyes, I envied.   I grew to resent the colors that set me apart from my family" (15).   The narrator notes that when she was four, "my sisters convinced me I was adopted. Eyes so green, this was not my family" (15).   Consequently, she considers (and later attempts) to fragment her own body, believing she might identify with her family if she can change her appearance: "At five, I took a butcher knife, sat calmly, sadly, on the pink chenille bedspread, threatening to slice away at tanned skin" (15).   Later she explains in detail the self-mutilation she experiences as a child, and this passage of bodily wounding is so significant that I quote it in full:

Self-inflicted wounds marked me at an early age. At four, I chewed my fingernails. I won't repress the habit. I relish it still. I bite nails and peel back cuticles until I draw blood. Raw chewed skin covered with drying blood, fingers layered with scabs. My thumbs throb where the cuts separate the nail from the skin. With short sharp nails, I pick back thick cuticle skin. Blood oozes from my thin fingers. The blunt weapons will grow for a week, then, I chew the thumbnails and the middle fingers with my teeth, spitting out particles. I leave the forefinger on one hand long to cut skin. The faces are fat and stubby. Physical pain will test me, excite me even. At eight I learned to take a sharp razor cutting designs on the heels of my feet, roughly shaping triangles, squiggles. I hated my feet. Blood still cakes the callused skin. I peel back pale, thin calluses, then cut underneath exposing pink flesh. Scars brand my heels. I anesthetize myself with pain. Blood oozes from my hands and feet. (71-72)

Here we discover that wounds may be inflicted not only by historical oppressions, such as those of *Beloved*'s Sethe, *Dictée*'s Yu Guan Soon, *Stigmata*'s Lizzie DuBose, or *Corregidora*'s Ursa, but also by the traumatized women themselves. Moreover, this passage complicates the symbol of the scar, for we find that scars are not always symbols of healing, as they may be for Sethe or Lizzie. In fact, these scars are symbols of an ongoing pain, for the narrator of *Gulf Dreams* indicates that this self-mutilation still occurs in the present day when she switches suddenly from past to present tense in the above passage. Also interesting is that the narrator's pain and suffering is, like Lizzie's suffering, likened to the wounds of Christ, or stigmata, in the last line of the passage. Thus, while the narrator's wounds are similar on some levels to the wounds of characters we have already examined, they are also unique because they have been self-inflicted, showing a much different kind of oppression.

Although she notes that it is during childhood that she begins to hate her body—since she fears she is unlike her family—the narrator's animosity toward her body is only exacerbated as she enters puberty: "For months, soft curls have begun to poke through underwear. I've wanted to shave, assuming I shouldn't. But, in the night once, I snuck a razor into bed to slice tender skin, leaving a scar. Now, my hair grows out prickly" (41). The narrator has a difficult time adjusting to her own body, struggling with elements of her own identity and body for reasons unknown to her until her teenage years. At fifteen years of age, however, the narrator discovers why it is that she feels such unease with her body. The narrator discovers that she is in love with a young woman.

Significantly, unlike most of the novels in this study, it is not the protagonist's mother who is mentioned on the novel's first page, but rather, in *Gulf Dreams*, "the young woman from El Pueblo" (11). This young woman is never given a name, and the authorial choice here is explained when the narrator states that to name her lover would "fetter you from all you embody" (139). I interpret this statement to mean that the nameless woman is an embodiment of the various oppressions endured by women of ethnic, racial, and sexual minorities. As Butler notes in *Undoing Gender*, "Sexuality does not follow from gender in the sense that what gender you 'are' determines what kind of sexuality you will 'have'" (16), yet heteronormativity still demands that sexuality should follow naturally from gender. Accordingly, this nameless woman, who attempts to hide her orientation behind a veil of convention, represents the story of innumerable, unnamable women. The girls' fateful meeting in adolescence prefigures the ongoing unease with their bodies and identities that they will continue to face.

Despite her evident love for the narrator, the nameless young woman attempts to shroud herself in convention, and convention ultimately rules when the young woman "gave in, chose a common, predictable life" (121). As the narrator notes, "She and I, trapped in social circumstances. Propriety kept us apart" (28). Eventually, the young woman from El Pueblo marries Pelón, a male lawyer. Of course, the narrator feels utterly betrayed by the young woman's marriage, and not only because of the women's evident love for each other. First, as she notes, by age fifteen, the narrator feels that "[m]en and deception became one fused reality" when she learns that her two older sisters' husbands are unfaithful (19). Second, although the narrator loves her father (19), she finds in her other relationships with men, particularly the white boy from Alabama, that "[m]aleness" is "convinced of its superiority to the feminine" (22). Moreover, the narrator discovers that men can cause jealousy and competition between women. For example, after the young women's first meeting, a year passes before they see each other. Then, when the narrator sees her again, the young woman "ached for me when I pranced with the boy from Alabama" (27). The young woman's jealousy underlines her desire for the narrator, and the competitions in which they engage foreshadow the inevitable.

As young adults, the women's desire for one another increases, and their relationship becomes much more convoluted until its hasty end. During the first year of junior college, during which they are roommates, they deepen their passionate relationship: "We reached new intimacies, beyond high school when we delighted in addictive passion [....] Our boyfriends, confused and angry, left us to each other" (53). Unfortunately for both women, the young woman will soon, according to the narrator, "dodge her own truth" (53). In their second year of junior college, the young woman meets Pelón, a Mexican pre-law student, and soon after, she leaves the narrator for him (62). After the young woman's retreat, when she "dodge[s]" her feelings, the narrator and the young woman do not see each other for many years. In the meantime, the bereft narrator "instigated suicide with cheap wine and diet pills," eventually becoming addicted to speed (45-46). The young woman "wait[s]," according to the narrator, until "after I left to commit herself to a hypocrite's ceremony" (47). Just as the young woman had envied the narrator's boyfriends, the narrator becomes enormously jealous of Pelón. But importantly, this feeling is deeper than envy; more poignantly, the narrator detests the ownership the young woman's husband assumes: "Her husband owned her, sapping her, wanting every piece of her, expecting what he'd had as a child. He held her frantically. His possession" (46). This passage aptly suggests that this marriage is entered into as an assumed, expected relationship in which a woman's identity is subsumed under a man's. Hence, while the narrator is jealous of Pelón, she is also cynical of heterosexual unions due to her distrust of men and her own love for the young woman.

When the women reunite, the young woman has been married for nearly a decade. But the hollowness of her marriage is represented by the "empty baby crib" (47), which is symbolic specifically in its refusal to provide the conventional life the young woman seeks. She has attempted to obtain a heterosexual union and children as products of her union. But the "hollow baby crib, this infertile life" (50) suggests that the young woman's choice has been made for the wrong reasons. As the two women visit for the first time in years at the young woman's and Pelón's home, the narrator notes, "The young woman had loved me, but my love wasn't enough. He had given her what I could not" (55). The suggestion here is that the narrator could not provide the young woman with the social acceptance of conventional, heteronormative family life. But after a decade of marriage, the young woman "admired my [the narrator's] freedom from her choices, her panacea had worn off, a foundation crumbled beneath her" (55). In other words, the young woman appreciates that the narrator did not choose convention, for the young woman has found, in fact, that her own façade has failed.

Gulf Dreams's **Fractured Bodies**

What is interesting, particularly in light of the narrator's childhood compulsion to wound herself, is the desire of these two women to wound each other. As noted earlier, the narrator is obsessed with self-mutilation, and a telling dream in adulthood indicates her ongoing obsession with wounding:

> When I sleep, I don't dream of you, there are no dreams of you to comfort me at night. Only nightmares, blood-drenched, nightmares. An axe swings, lands on my back, splits me open, my spine breaks. My skull fractured, brains spill on concrete, blood flows, I'm emptied out. Depleted. Now I'll have serenity. My mind won't be muddled or ensnared with you. I'm emptied of a brain to be clear again. But recurring visions bring no shelter. There is no peace when I sleep. (144)

The dream reflects both the wounding the narrator inflicted on herself as a child and the wounding of each other in which the women engage.

When the young woman begins dating Pelón in college, she discovers the psychological power struggle that so often characterizes heterosexual relationships. Ostensibly to convince herself that a lesbian relationship would be equally problematic, the young woman immediately rushes to the narrator in order to learn if the narrator, too, will hurt her. As the narrator states, the young woman "believ[ed] she deserved punishment" (62). Indeed, the young woman suffered abuse in her childhood, and the narrator believes that she consequently plays the "victim's role" (28). But I would add that the young woman is trying to determine whether or not the heteronormative union is essentially better. As the narrator says, "The young woman needed assurance that I was like him, that I would also punish her, believing she deserved punishment" (62). Clearly, the young woman's retreat into convention has provided her with an undesirable power structure; consequently, her desire to be hurt by the narrator assures her that the lesbian relationship is not a better alternative.

Indeed, this assurance becomes a "savage game" in which the women violently fragment each other's bodies: "I hit her, tightening my grip around her arm, bruising the skin, leaving purple blotches. I wanted to clutch her, to own her. I could only reach her with cruelty" (63). The game backfires, however, when Pelón also hits the young woman. While the narrator comforts the young woman, kissing a bruise, she also notes later that "I compound her purple marks. She is satisfied to hate me. I couldn't stop. Nor could she" (63). The word "hate" shows that this game works—that the young woman is convinced that a lesbian relationship is equally as painful as her "conventional" life with Pelón. In return, the young woman also takes pleasure in hurting the narrator, perhaps to demonstrate her "hate," or more likely, to try to deny her love for the narrator: "She wanted to wound me. I cried for her touch, any touch [....] I recreated her greed, listening in my head to words she spoke, that she was in love. The words, like abuse" (62). These words voice the young woman's sexual and romantic experiences, which are as painful as bodily violence to the narrator: "[S]he narrates scenes that strike like blows. Spilling portions of sexual technique, forcing me to listen [....] The young woman paralyzes me, then attacks. It was, I'm sure, her pleasure" (64). The reader appropriately asks how this violent, jealous, and competitive relationship could possibly be a better alternative than a heterosexual partnership. In fact, the women have begun a cycle that serves a dual purpose. First, it helps the women assure themselves that a lesbian relationship is no less painful than a hetero-union. In other words, this violence is used by the women—if subconsciously—to convince them that their relationship is not, in fact, a viable option. Second, the fighting also helps the narrator to accept the impending break with the young woman. The narrator becomes increasingly aware, of course, that this relationship will not last, that the young woman from El Pueblo will inevitably retreat into a more conventional life with Pelón.

The second section of *Gulf Dreams* tells the story of a young Chicana woman, Ermila, who is gang-raped and whose case ultimately goes to court—a subplot that reinforces the novel's overarching critiques of patriarchy and heteronormativity. The plots intersect when Pelón defends Ermila's rapists. In the decade that has passed, however, the tension between the women has only increased. Instead of a loving and nurturing reunion, the two women find themselves again corporeally fragmenting one another. The scenes in which this violence occurs are tragic:

> I bit her tongue. Maliciously, I bit again, harder. Her hand, stroking my hair, clenched a fist, and yanked hard. My head jerked back, blood trickled from her wound to my bottom lip. She wiped the blood with her thumb, confused, injured, but not angry. (108)

This violence echoes what I have been arguing throughout this study. The bodily fragmentation that occurs here is a result of social oppressions that normalize certain behaviors. But unlike *Beloved*, *Dictée*, *Stigmata*, and *Corregidora*, the wounds are not inflicted by historical oppressions, but rather by the women themselves. The reader can see that a recognition of these shared wounds, products of heteronormativity, would provide the women with means of understanding and perhaps healing. Unfortunately, heteronormative demands keep these women from the connections that would heal them.

In the central and climactic scene of bodily fragmentation, the two women finally fight. During the trial, the narrator stays at her brother's house, and one evening, the young woman unexpectedly visits. The narrator has been appalled that the young woman can tolerate Pelón while he defends Ermila's brutal rapists, but she is also overwhelmed by her own passion for the young woman. Immediately when the young woman arrives, "[j]ealousy overcame" the narrator, who notes that she "wanted to possess her" (108). As the young woman looks at a childhood picture of the narrator, the narrator feels "angry she's here" (109). Then, when the young woman kisses the narrator with a "savage kiss," the narrator bites her tongue, painfully drawing blood. A horrific and bloody fight ensues: "[A] woman shrieks, screeching louder, pounding on a back with clenched fists. A precise rage. Moving closer to slap, to choke, kicking a living room chair, grabbing photographs two at a time from a wall, smashing them" (109). The young woman hurls the childhood photographs she was looking at a few moments earlier. Then, the narrator runs out the door and into the night when "[g]lass flies. A piece lodges on a left forearm [....] Red blood drips round spots on the sidewalk, leaving a trail" (109-10).

I argue that this episode is the central scene of bodily fragmentation in a novel full of fragmented bodies. The scene brilliantly represents the feminist repercussions of bodily wounding and scarring that I want to emphasize. When the narrator bites the young woman's tongue, the young woman becomes so enraged that she destroys the narrator's childhood pictures. Because it is specifically a childhood photograph that is shattered, a piece of which lodges in the narrator's arm, we must consider its significance. The picture is that of the narrator and her brother. Therefore, childhood memories, as represented by the photograph, physically *become* the wound. In other words, the young woman wounds the narrator using the weapon of childhood memories.

We can read these memories in several ways. One way might be to recall the childhood days the girls spent together when their love seemed pure (remembering that they were just fifteen years old at their first meeting). Hence, painful emotions are evoked at the memories of the time they spent together prior to their compulsion toward heteronormative expectations.

Another way to read the memories is to recall the pain in both women's lives:

> Childhood scars were temporal wounds, invisible reminders, but [...] as visible as branded flesh, like a burn from cooking, the direct contact with fire stings swiftly, but the scar from the burn is marked on skin, a reminder of things forgotten. (98)

In fact, "childhood scars" mark many of these women. The narrator describes (though not to the young woman) her childhood abuses by men: "Boys, cousins, uncles had pawed me. No one suspected. I wanted to tell her. But I didn't" (61). Likewise, the young woman, too, endures childhood abuse: "[T]he young woman from El Pueblo blurted out how her step-father groped her young girl's breasts for years [...] when her mother was at work. He began when she was a little girl, eight or nine" (60-61). These women have similar childhood memories, but the narrator's refusal to reciprocate her stories with the young woman disallows a sharing of wounds and consequent healing. On the other hand, the women silently understand each other, and their oppressions remain one area in which they do not compete: "I couldn't compete with her past, nor could she with mine. There was no competition, only commonality" (27). Hence, even though they do not discuss these traumatic histories, there is some understanding of shared histories.

These silent, shared oppressions may be why, as the narrator flees her brother's house with glass lodged in her arm, the young woman chases her, "clutches an injured arm and tugs me back to my brother's house," and then proceeds to "treat the injury" (110). Hence, the scene involves a purposeful and symbolic fragmentation of bodies, but it culminates in an even more significant scene of healing:

> Words are not spoken. She leads me into the bathroom where she finds tweezers, iodine, and gauze to treat the injury. As she pulls the thin, sharp glass from my arm's soft underside, my tears flow as easily as the blood spurting from my flesh. (110)

Though the wounds have been inflicted by the young woman, she also recognizes them as shared wounds, inflicted largely by their inability to maintain a meaningful relationship. Even more interesting than this attempt to heal a shared wound is the subversive victory the young woman exhibits. For during this cleansing and healing process, "The young woman licks my arm [...] smearing her cheeks, then my mouth, up and down; chin, lips, forehead are dabbed and anointed. She is pleased with her victory, a crimson victory, self-satisfied to eye longing on my face" (110). The young woman's sense of victory may emerge for various reasons. One possibility is that the young woman, physically abused and wounded first by her step-father, then by Pelón, and finally by the narrator herself, finally feels victory in fragmenting others. Another possibility is that she feels victory in *sharing* these wounds with the narrator. In other words, both women are oppressed and repressed, and they struggle to express their similar experiences. Here, a wound becomes something empathetically experienced by both women, and this moment of mutual understanding allows for a brief victory. And a third possibility is that the young woman senses victory in being able to *heal* the wound. While the two women have been fragmented by heteronormative communities, they are also capable of healing these shared wounds, bringing a feeling of empowerment to the young woman.

Despite the young woman's attempt to heal the narrator, the narrator still "hated her" (110)—not because of the violence of that night, but because the young woman's husband, Pelón, continues to defend Ermila's rapists—and the young woman seems to have no compunction: "Throughout the trial, I hated her. She, with her husband and his rapists, so proud, refusing to reclaim Ermila" (110). Ermila's rape takes place fifteen years after the young woman and the narrator meet as girls. The newspaper account states that there are five rapists, most of them young. (Four of them are between sixteen and twenty-five years old.) As she reads the account, the narrator imagines the rape of Ermila:

> I imagined this. Saw them drive up in a banged up beige Ford Galaxy, pull her in from the side of the road where she strolled at dusk to her *abuelita*'s. Four men thrust her into the back seat. The driver keeps the engine running. I imagine her terror. They finish raiding her, drive back to the road where they found her, push her out of the back seat; she rolls down an embankment, grassy, dry from the day's heat. No one would view her lying in a ditch. She regains consciousness, stands up, fumbles with a ripped skirt and flees to her grandmother's, her body aching. (78)

Ermila's fragmented body is wounded physically and psychologically: "Her bruises, internal, her skin unscathed, the police would lie. She is scarred inner flesh" (78). Her story embodies the experience of many raped women; many, of course, never tell their stories, but others, like Ermila, attempt to receive justice in court.

However, her community, including many women, urge Ermila not to press charges: "They tried to censor her anger. The compassion some offered was not compassion at all, but instead words meant to stifle her" (89). On the other hand, it is Ermila's grandmother who, like *Beloved*'s Baby Suggs, cares for Ermila: "[O]nly her *güelita* listened and repaired her broken flesh the night she stumbled in wailing at her abductors" (89-90). Her grandmother further insists that women must fight for justice: "Ermila's *güelita* insisted sometimes one had to shout, to thunder cries for all to hear because if a woman didn't roar at injustice, a day would come when all would be taken from her" (91-92). Unfortunately, most of the town sides against Ermila, for according to Pelón's defense of the rapists, it is the men who are "victims," and Ermila got "what she wanted" (93). Regardless, Ermila's grandmother "gave Ermila quiet encouragement to fight a town's conscience, one that wanted her censored" (92). As the narrator notes, "The town stifled loud, irreverent women, women expected to stay in their place, to spoil men, to listen to their troubles," for a "woman's strength was judged by how she accepted her husband, no matter what kind of life he dealt her, drunkenness, womanizing, a slap or a firm word" (92). In other words, the psychological and physical fragmentation of women is not only accepted, but encouraged in this patriarchal community, though the healing and nurturing of strong women such as Ermila and her grandmother allow for some women to resist.

Ermila's bodily fragmentation thus becomes the symbol for the kind of patriarchal damage done to the women of this town. Sadly, Ermila's fragmented flesh becomes "deadened, could not respond to contact anymore," and as the narrator asks, "How do you recreate loving touch and memory when repulsion ruptures the body, the psyche" (78). When Pelón calls the rapist a "victim," the narrator points out that "[t]he woman is absent, a consequence. Her injury is nothing to these men who decide she is their whore" (93). Ermila's fragmented body is central to my claim that the fragmented gendered, racialized body is an indicator of oppression but also a connective force between women of shared experiences. Ermila's story provides a poignant final emphasis of my argument that the fragmented female body is representative of historical and social oppressions. Like the narrator and the young woman from El Pueblo, Ermila's body becomes the site on which these social and patriarchal oppressions are etched. The support provided by Ermila's grandmother contrasts with the troubled relationship between the young woman and the narrator, yet both cases demonstrate the fragmentations of patriarchal and heteronormative societies as well as the healing that comes with women's bonds.

Ultimately, *Gulf Dreams* ends on a pessimistic yet resistant note. After the young woman concedes that she disagrees with her husband's defense of the rapists (117), Pelón threatens the narrator, knowing that his wife desires her (126), and contact between the women ends. Eventually, the narrator leaves El Pueblo and goes to Los Angeles. She never reunites with the young woman, though "she, the young woman, came with me. Every night, in dreams" (129). The narrator dreams and thinks of the young woman constantly, and she fails to find a fulfilling relationship elsewhere. Even though her experience is hauntingly painful, I argue that *Gulf Dreams* is strongly feminist and resistant, largely because it critiques the heteronormative and patriarchal standards that lead the narrator into this devastating situation. The reader can see the young woman's love for the narrator, even as the young woman fearfully withdraws into a "conventional" way of life. When the two women violently fight and fragment each other's bodies, we see that they are attempting to overcome their love for one another, and to convince themselves that a relationship with each other would be painful and dangerous, just as a heterosexual partnership is. In the end, *Gulf Dreams* demonstrates, through the denial of female connection, the resistance that strong relationships between women could provide.

The Woman Who Owned the Shadows
and the Denial of Lesbian Love

Like Pérez's *Gulf Dreams*, Allen's *The Woman Who Owned the Shadows* portrays the relationship of two adolescent lovers who separate due to societal constraints. Similar to the other novels in this study, the narrative style is highly fragmented, shifting between Ephanie's contemporary story and traditional Guadalupe stories. In fact, much of the action seems to occur not in the movement of the plot itself, which is driven largely by Ephanie's travels between New Mexico and San Francisco, but within Ephanie's mind as she searches for a lost identity. The protagonist is Ephanie Kawiemie Atencio, whose struggle to reclaim identity is at the center of the novel. Ephanie feels that her name matches her fragmented racial identity, and I comment further on the significance of her name. An uncommon name, Ephanie feels that her name might have been "Epiphany" or "Effie" (3). But I suggest that "Ephanie" also connotes a similar and far more common name, Stephanie. What is omitted from Stephanie, however, are the letters "S" and "t," or "St," a shorthand for both "street" and "saint." The name, hence, may suggest either a loss of direction or the inability for sainthood. Interestingly, both of these readings are upheld in the novel. Ephanie travels to various places, looking for an element of self that she feels she has lost. Also, she learns of her inability for Christian salvation when she learns at the mission school that her relationship is "the devil" and "a sin" (30).

Ephanie and childhood friend Elena, a Chicana girl from a neighboring town, spend every day together, and as they enter their teenage years, they realize that they are becoming lovers. When Elena's mother tells her that she must stop spending time with Ephanie, Ephanie's developing understanding of herself is destroyed. The lesbian relationship they are entering is condemned by their social and religious communities, though consequent attempts at heterosexual unions lead to feelings of losing direction—as is reflected in Ephanie's name.

After the loss of her deepening relationship with Elena, whom she ostensibly never sees again after adolescence, Ephanie attempts, like the narrator and the young woman of *Gulf Dreams*, to live an "acceptable" heterosexual life. When we meet Ephanie in the opening pages, she is newly out of a marriage to a man about whom we learn little. Ephanie simply notes that this was a "cruel marriage" to a "man who left one night, late, into the rain slanting down around him, his small-brimmed stetson pulled tight over his skull [....] Who had gone then. Left. Her. And the babies" (8). We discover little about this marriage, though we have suspicions about its end. Ephanie notes that this was a "cruel marriage" (8), but she does not clarify whether the man himself was angry or violent, or whether it is the convention of marriage that is cruel. It is possible that the marriage ends because this husband, like Ursa's husbands Mutt and Tadpole in *Corregidora*, senses Ephanie's lack of passion for men. Another possibility, of course, is that this husband, like Pelón in *Gulf Dreams*, senses that Ephanie is being untrue to herself—that she, like the young woman from El Pueblo, is in fact pressured into marriage. And of course, it is possible that this husband is abusive or unfaithful, for Ephanie thinks to herself, "He'll never do it to anyone else. She vowed. She swore" (9). Allen's choice to omit further details on the marriage is intriguing, but in any case, we know only that the marriage ends and that Ephanie continues her quest for identity.

Sending her two children, Agnes and Ben, to stay with her parents, Ephanie embarks on a lengthy process of healing that involves first a disturbing romantic bout with her longtime friend Stephen, a fair-skinned "Indian cousin, friend, dear as a brother," though not related by blood (8). The relationship is problematic because Stephen takes advantage of Ephanie's psychological state, telling her, "You need me to take care of you [....] You know you need me to. You are so weak, now. I will take care of you, little one, sister. I will take care of you" (9). In her devastation,

Ephanie "did not realize that it was he who told her often, every day, more, that she would surely die without him to secure her, to make her self" (10). He convinces her that she needs his help with parenting as well: "She was helpless, he said. The blow to her. The mothering. She could not do. He said it. She silent, sick and exhausted, believed" (10). Interestingly, even while Ephanie carries on this relationship with Stephen, she thinks to herself, "I hate him" (10), and she notes that she wants him to leave (11). We begin to see an underlying, conflicted feeling toward Stephen, though we learn much more at the novel's end.

When she eventually escapes this relationship, Ephanie moves to San Francisco, where she meets Teresa, a white woman, at a therapy group. This woman soon becomes a close friend and perhaps lover of Ephanie's, a companionship that lasts for many years. During this time, Ephanie marries for a second time, this time to Thomas Yoshuri, a Niesei man to whom Ephanie seems attracted solely because he "needed her" (94). Ephanie learns of the oppressions that have faced Japanese Americans, oppressions which haunt Thomas. Ephanie, therefore, feels she can finally take the role of healer, though this role will not last. Shortly after their marriage, the couple has twins, Tommy and Tsali; sadly, Tommy dies shortly after his birth. To overcome their grief, Thomas, Teresa, and the three children, Agnes, Ben, and the infant Tsali, travel to the beach. But rather than overcome her grief for the lost infant, Ephanie instead comes to a realization about her marriage to Thomas. While swimming in the ocean, Ephanie feels herself being pulled by the tide out to sea. As she moves slowly away from the shoreline, she realizes she may die. But when Thomas realizes she is being pulled out to sea, he runs—not toward her to help—but away from her. Importantly, it is Teresa who saves Ephanie, quickly and easily transporting her from the current to more shallow water where Ephanie can stand again. Reflecting on this episode later that evening, Ephanie has an epiphany:

> That night, lying still in the dark, breathing, in her mind back home and in childhood safe Ephanie remembered something, about Elena. A hand to help her across a long jump on the mesas. She knew something then. Something she did not say aloud. Something true. (108)

She realizes that Thomas, an oppressed and frustrated man himself, has displaced much of his rage onto his wife, leaving her to be carried away as a symbol of his oppressors. Paradoxically, while seeing Ephanie as the embodiment of his oppression, Thomas conversely has become the oppressor, nearly allowing Ephanie to die. Moreover, in this moment of realization, Ephanie recalls that Elena had often, in childhood, reached out a helping hand to Ephanie as they climbed rocks and trees and crossed the mesas. By allowing her to drift to sea, Thomas sets himself in distinct contrast to Elena, who would never have allowed Ephanie to get hurt. When Ephanie contrasts these two people, her husband and her childhood love, she begins to realize her own misconceptions about Elena, and she begins to understand Elena's role in her identity.

Ephanie's Fragmented Body

This epiphany begins to help Ephanie understand the central conflict of the novel: a painful, childhood incident in which Ephanie's body and identity are simultaneously broken. Like *Gulf Dreams*'s painful central scene, this incident is a climactic moment. In this incident, which gradually comes back to Ephanie over the course of the novel, Stephen dares Ephanie to jump from a rope in the symbolic apple tree where Ephanie and Elena often spend time. Slowly, Ephanie begins to realize that it was not Elena who asked her to jump. Although she remembers Elena saying, "Fall," Elena had actually said, "Don't fall," and had told Ephanie the dare was far too dangerous (202). Later in the novel, Ephanie fully recalls that it was Stephen who told her to jump: "'Jump' [....] *He* had said that. She remembered" (191, emphasis added). Sadly, Ephanie's body is painfully mangled in this fall:

> [C]oming to again, lying on a board that some men were carrying, her father among them [....] They took her to Albuquerque, to the hospital. They said she'd broken two ribs and punctured a lung and it had collapsed. They drained the fluid that had collected there with a longlong needle and a terrifyinghuge syringe. They said soothing things to her. They said she was lucky she didn't break her neck. (202)

This event, the central scene in the novel, comes at the novel's end. The fragmented body becomes symbolic on many levels, and it specifically critiques those heteronormative demands that will soon tear Ephanie and Elena from one another.

Following a suicide attempt in adulthood, Ephanie clearly recalls the moment she fell from the tree. She poignantly reflects on the injury to her body and her identity caused by this incident:

> "All those years," she said to the deep shadows that clung to the room. "All those years and I never realized what had happened." And now she knew. That what she

had begun had never been completed. Because she fell she had turned her back on herself. Had misunderstood thoroughly the significance of the event. Had not even seen that she had been another sort of person before she fell. "I abandoned myself," she said. "I left me." And began to laugh, realizing. To laugh as all the memories came flooding back. Herself cartwheeling through the village. Whooping and hollering as she and Elena galloped their horses along the dusty road, practicing with their ropes to send the whirling loops sailing over the heads of the placid cows who wandered freely on the reservation lands. I was going to be a hero, before I got sidetracked, she thought. I was going to be full of life and action. I wasn't going to be the one who lived alone, afraid of the world. Elena and I, we were going to do brave things in our lives. And we were going to do them together. (204)

Ephanie realizes that she negated her identity when she listened to Stephen and jumped from the tree. Moreover, Thomas's lack of heroism (when he fails to rescue Ephanie from the ocean) catalyzes Ephanie's realization that she and Elena *were* in fact brave, that Elena was in fact the hero in Ephanie's life. After Ephanie's fall, "The old ease with her body was gone" (202). After the fall, she begins to dream of "being tall and pretty and dated. Adored. Mated. Housed in some pretty house somewhere far from the dusty mesas of her childhood [....] Someplace nice. With vacuum cleaners and carpets and drapes" (203). Ephanie's rejection of her "tomboy" qualities in favor of traditional female roles echoes the definition of heteronormativity given by Catherine Rottenberg, who argues, "Subjects are encouraged to desire to live up to the norms of a specific gender while concomitantly encouraged (and compelled) to desire the other [....] By compelling *and encouraging* 'women' to live up to norms of femininity and 'men' to attempt to embody masculinity, heteronormative regimes reinforce their hegemony" (441-42, italics in original). Indeed, Ephanie now adheres to the advice her community has been giving her—that she should act more like a lady.

As Ephanie recovers these fragmentary memories, she also recalls Native American cultural stories, presented as brief vignettes throughout the novel. These stories, told by her grandmother, force Ephanie to fill in the gaps between stories and to understand her place in her culture: "Her grandma used to tell her stories [....] She often thought she had already said them, so she would not finish them or would say only a piece of them. Leaving Ephanie, the child, to make those pieces whole" (79). Tara Prince-Hughes argues that Ephanie's search for identity, in fact, revolves more around her ability to recognize herself as a "cultural preserver and a teller of stories" than around her acceptance of her sexual identity (15). While I believe her sexual identity is of greater import than does Prince-Hughes, it is true that Ephanie is responsible for perpetuating her people's stories, for the mythical

Spider Grandmother tells her, "Your place in the great circling spiral is to help in that story, in that work. To pass on to those who can understand what you have learned, what you know" (210). The Grandmother beckons Ephanie to tell Teresa: "Give it to your sister, Teresa. The one who waits. She is ready to know" (210). Likewise, Vanessa Holford eloquently argues that "Ephanie's return to the creation stories of the Grandmother means a rediscovery of her self: a reconciliation with the body, a renewed ability for twinning, and a new realization of feminine power" (106). I agree with Holford's observation here, for Ephanie's (re)connection to her matrilineal history allows her to connect with women in her contemporary world. But I suggest that Ephanie must heal other damages first.

Before Ephanie realizes her role as cultural transmitter, she must, like the other women in this study, find a way to repair her fragmented identity, which has been silenced and oppressed by virtue of Ephanie's gender, sexual identity, and ethnicity:

> She knew it had to come together. To knit in an invisible seam. To become whole, entire. In her thought. Her mind. Separation was against the Law. The one that the sun rose by. The one that let the water sing. Inside and outside must meet, she knew, desperately. Must cohere. Equilibrate. (174)

This need for wholeness reflects Ephanie's position in a Western world of binaries and hierarchies. In *Stigmata*, Lizzie DuBose notes that life is circular (94), and Ephanie similarly notes that "Indians lived in circles, did not care for lines that broken went nowhere" (185). In a parallel critique of Western divisions and linearity, one chapter title in Allen's novel is "What Is Divided In Two Brings War" (189). These statements are reflective of a need for coherence, not fragmentation, for a world characterized by the equality of the circle, not that of the hierarchical line. Unfortunately, there is no way around a fragmentary language and life for many Native Americans, who are forced to live on reservations set up by whites and to speak the very language that has served to oppress them. As Ephanie notes, the English language is a key source of oppression and cultural fragmentation:

> But the words she had. The language wasn't built for truth. It was a lying tongue. The only one she had. It made separations. Divided against itself. It could not allow enwholement. Only fragmentation. And it was the only language they all knew together—the people in her world [....] The only containers for the food, the water, the soil of recovery, uncovery, discovery. To re learn. To re member. To put back what had been shattered. To re mind. To re think. The beginning so as to grasp the end [....] And all the fragments of all the shattered hearts gathered

carefully into one place. Tenderly cared for. Would grow. That truth. The one where all the waters would come together. Shipap. The Mother's home. The place of the one good heart. (190)

This telling passage details the language that has so fragmented the Native American culture. As Ephanie points out, English is a language of division. She notes the difficulty with which Native Americans tell their history in the English language. Another interesting point in this passage is the idea that "[t]he Mother's home" is the place of enwholement. In one dream, a katsina shows Ephanie Shipap: "the origin. The place of the mother. Shipap. The place of memory, the place of dream. The place where all rain, all knowledge, all connection comes from. The place that first and finally is home" (130). Like Theresa Hak Kyung Cha's *Dictée*, in which "your mother" is equated with "your home" (49), wholeness here is found only in the mother's home.

Women's Bonds in *The Woman Who Owned the Shadows*

As with the other novels in this study, Ephanie's fragmentation, which arises from various sources (patriarchy, racism, classism, heteronormativity) can be contested through women's bonds. Like several novels in this study dedicated to mothers, grandmothers, and great-grandmothers, *The Woman Who Owned the Shadows* is dedicated to "my great grandmother, Meta Atseye Gunn." The novel is also dedicated "To Naiya Iyatiku," Ephanie's clan mother, and "to Spider Grandmother, Thought Woman, who thinks the stories I write down." These three dedications indicate the significance that ethnicity will play in the novel, for Ephanie's cultural foremothers are as important in this dedication as are her biological foremothers. Moreover, by dedicating the novel to these various mothers, the author indicates the significance of remembering and revering one's matrilineage. Likewise, the characters understand the importance of celebrating matrilineage, for Ephanie's mother tells the stories that her mother used to tell her (69). As she does so, Ephanie realizes, "She looked just like Grandma Campbell then, laughing like the old Indian ladies everywhere laughed [....] Like two girls they [Ephanie and her mother] giggled and hummed in mutual recognition of Grandma's penetrating thought, her wit" (70). Ephanie wonders whether her grandmother, Shimanna (Nightshade), who was given a European name (Sylvia) and sent to a mission school, felt whole, or whether she, too, was fragmented: "She was a Presbyterian, but she never entirely lost her heathen ways. Did she reconcile the differences, or was she cut in two?" (149). Ephanie notes that it was so offensive to the Native American clans for a member to marry a white person that her grandmother, who married a white man, was not given a traditional burial, and her offspring were not accepted by the other villagers.

It is because of this displacement in her community that Ephanie befriends Elena. Like *Gulf Dreams*'s narrator and the young woman from El Pueblo, who become lovers in adolescence, Ephanie and Elena become inseparable friends in childhood, and they are forced apart by their heteronormative religious and social communities when they reach puberty, or an age, presumably, when they can become lovers. The novel's first mention of Elena occurs in a dream that Ephanie has early in the novel, a dream that occurs when she is in a state of depression and confusion after her husband leaves her. The abandonment by this man triggers memories of Elena that readers receive in small glimpses as dreams or memories. Elena's first appearance, this dream, involves "Elena, amiga, tiny girls running in frantic circles around her grandmother's house, screaming" (6). Following this first mention, Elena is an enigmatic but clearly central character, whose connection to Ephanie is given in brief vignettes as Ephanie recalls their childhood together.[26] One prominent and telling symbol is the apple tree where Ephanie and Elena spend time together. We learn that the two girls have a loving relationship: "It had been the apple tree. The long spring days there. With the girl. They had watched the village going. They had watched the clouds" (21). The blossoming springtime apple tree, of course, coincides with the blossoming love of the two girls.

Interestingly, as mentioned earlier, we also learn that the girls do not fit the conventional roles of young girls in this community:

> They had ridden horses, pretending to be ranchers, chasing the village cattle around the town, they suffered scoldings for it. They learned to be trick riders. Roy Rogers and Hopalong Cassidy. Maybe they could be stunt men in Hollywood if they got good enough at it, if they could learn to jump from the rooftop onto the horse's back. They had chased the clouds. (21-22)

Indeed, the girls spend most of their time outdoors doing things that only boys, in this community, typically do. And as the girls grow, their lives are increasingly entangled with one another's. One passage summarizes their loving relationship, beyond differences, so well that I quote it at length:

> In their seasons they grew. Walking the road between their houses, lying langorous [sic] and innocent in the blooming boughs of the apple tree. Amid the fruiting

limbs. And had known themselves and their surroundings in terms of each other's eyes. Though their lives were very different, their identity was such that the differences were never strange. They had secret names for each other, half joking, half descriptive, Snow White and Rose Red, they named themselves [...] In recognition also of the closeness they shared, those friends [....] All those years, in spite of distance, in spite of difference, in spite of change, they understood the exact measure of their relationship, the twining, the twinning. There were photographs of them from that time. Because Elena's gold-tinged hair looked dark in the photograph's light, no one could say which was Elena, which Ephanie. With each other they were each one doubled. They were thus complete. (22)

The completeness that arises from their togetherness stands in stark contrast to the fragmentation that Ephanie later experiences in their separation. Their understanding and love for one another is clear; therefore, it becomes evident that some powerful events must have served to damage the relationship between them, though Ephanie's memories are vague until the end of the novel.

Though the girls spend their days together, playing and talking, the one thing they do not discuss is their blossoming romance and the prospect of adulthood: "Together they had dreamed. Sharing. They never talked about growing up. What that would mean" (21). "What that would mean," in this case, is heteronormativity and the prospect of marriage. In other words, the girls seem to realize that they will be driven away from each other if their relationship continues to develop. Ephanie recalls of the mission school she and Elena attend that the nuns had disapproved of the early homoerotic attractions between the girls. And Ephanie sadly recalls "that helpless day" when Elena repeats what one nun had said, "That evil made Ephanie and Elena play dirty things" (13). She says, "They should be ashamed. They should be afraid. They would have to go to confession about it if they kept on playing like that, between each other's legs when they were one or two years older and could sin" (13). Their early friendship develops, as the girls grow up, into a relationship that threatens the norms of the girls' societies.

Inevitably, the two girls are eventually torn apart by their heteronormative societies. The specific event marking their separation is their journey to the peak of Picacho, a tall rock formation in the middle of the plains. This dangerous climb is one the girls had anticipated for years. The peak has several legends tied to it—Elena's Chicano/a people and Ephanie's Guadalupe people have different stories about the peak, but interestingly, each story involves a woman jumping to her death. The story of the devastated woman who jumps—whether it is because of a lover who has died or because of a forbidden romance—foreshadows both the devastation Ephanie will experience atop the peak and her own fateful jump from the apple tree a few years earlier, an event of which readers do not learn until the end of the novel.

As they make the treacherous climb, we see both the risk and the safety their relationship provides, for during the dangerous climb, "Ephanie looked at Elena for reassurance, thinking how beautiful her friend was" (27). However, at the top of this significant peak, Elena breaks the news that will forever affect Ephanie: "I can't come over to your place anymore. Not ever. My mother says I can't see you at all" (28). In shock, Ephanie determines that the reason must be class-related, for Ephanie's family "had more. Of everything" (29). However, the reason, Elena explains, is "because my mother thinks we spend too much time with each other" (29). As reality dawns on her, Ephanie thinks, "How could she not see Elena? Be with her. Who would she be with then, if not Elena?" (29). In response to Ephanie's silence, Elena explains further, "You know [...] The way we've been lately. Hugging and giggling. You know." She notes, "I asked the sister about that, after school. She said it was the devil. That I mustn't do anything like that. That it was a sin. And she told my mother. She says I can't come over any more" (30). Clearly, Elena has been socialized to believe that the relationship she has with Ephanie is unacceptable. Therefore, she asks the nun at her school, who confirms Elena's suspicions and tells her mother. Receiving Elena's news, Ephanie does not respond, except to put her hand on Elena's arm, and silently, Ephanie considers jumping from the peak, much like the legendary Guadalupe or Chicana woman who had killed herself in a similar moment of desperation: "She [Ephanie] looked over the side of the peak and thought about flying. Dropping off. She thought of going to sleep" (29). Ephanie's devastation at this news—that she can no longer see her closest friend and love—is so deep that she considers suicide.

But Ephanie gradually realizes that Elena has simply seen the "problem" first. Ephanie "[u]nderstood, wordlessly, exactly what Elena was saying. How she could understand what Ephanie had not understood. That they were becoming lovers. That they were in love. That their loving had to stop. To end" (30). The relationship has "to end" because it is unacceptable within their religious, familial, ethnic, and social communities. As Elena notes, "I was scared. I thought it was wrong. It is" (30). Elena, in fact, has learned heteronorms. Her knowledge may stem from an incident at the mission school, when two nuns seem to fall in love; to the young students at the mission, this relationship seems perfectly harmonious and natural, until one nun is immediately and silently relocated (155). While Elena becomes afraid and begins to question her relationship with Ephanie, however, Ephanie herself has not prepared for the possible ending of the relationship; the news makes her feel "[t]hat she was falling. Had fallen. Would not recover from the fall, smashing, the rocks. That they were in her, not on the ground" (30). This metaphoric fall echoes the story of the woman who fell from the sky, the legend of the woman who jumps from Picacho, and the fall Ephanie takes from the symbolic apple tree.

Years later, as Ephanie attempts to distinguish memories from dreams, she finds that she intermittently remembers "that particular unknown event that she was dying of" (182). This memory, as we know, involves Ephanie's fall from the tree when Stephen dares her, at twelve years old, to jump. She continually remembers the words, "Jump" (4, 191) and "Jump. / Fall" (23, 31, 173, 211). Ephanie recalls that Elena always kept them safe, "Except for that one time that she hadn't kept them safe" (23). But Ephanie realizes much later in life that it was Stephen, not Elena, who asked her to jump. And the fall she takes effectively changes her life. After noting that she was "going to be a hero" and that she and Elena were going to do "brave things" together, she reflects on why this goal never happened:

> And what had happened to all of that? A fall, a serious fall. A conversation a few years later that ended her friendship with Elena. A fear, a running away, an abandonment. But I had already left myself before Elena abandoned me, she thought now. Because I thought I should have been smarter than to listen to Stephen's dare. Because I was hurt. Because I was in the hospital for a few days, alone and scared and feeling so guilty. So guilty I never trusted my own judgment, my own vision again. (205)

Ephanie blames herself for accepting Stephen's dare and for consequently becoming more "ladylike." Now, in the present, Ephanie thinks fondly of her childhood with Elena: "Elena and she walking. Lying on the grass making stories out of clouds. Climbing the endless mesas of her home. Talking for hours safe in the welcoming branches of the apple tree. Holding hands" (33). In her present life, Ephanie is "[t]rying to make a new friend. Who would be like Elena. A friend she could be safe and sure with. A friend who was like home" (33). The bonds that are "like home" are reminiscent of those seen in *Dictée*, in which Cha writes, "Your mother your home" (49). In remembering this scene correctly, in overturning "the long buried conviction Ephanie had harbored that Elena had made her fall," Ephanie "finally found again the ground" (205). By remembering the event that had drastically changed Ephanie's understanding of herself, she is finally able to move on.

It is largely heteronormativity that fragments and denies Ephanie's and Elena's identities in the first place. At several points, the adult Ephanie is still frustrated with her sexual identity: "[A] knowing what she was rose in her like lies, like filthy, like the once clean air now burdened everywhere with death" (132). She also calls some elements of her identity "the monstrous other in her," which she "wished she could tear out" (132). Though she fears admitting her latent lesbianism, she does realize that it is only in the sisterhood she obtains with Elena that she is "complete" (22). As Holford argues, "Ephanie needs to find her other half, to become whole, and for her this becomes possible with another woman" (105). Fortunately, this wholeness again becomes possible with Teresa. When the Grandmother tells Ephanie, "Give it [Ephanie's story] to your sister, Teresa. The one who waits. She is ready to know" (210), the novel emphasizes the completeness that comes with friendships between girls and women. Like *Gulf Dreams*, this novel does not end with a reunion. Rather, it ends with Ephanie's acceptance of her separation from Elena. However, Ephanie does find hope and fulfillment in her friendship with Teresa, in her recollection of the Grandmother's stories, and in her understanding of Elena's saving role in Ephanie's fall from the apple tree.

Overturning Western Dualities

Several of the heteronormative institutions to which the young woman from El Pueblo, the nameless narrator, Ephanie, and Elena are subjected arise from Western philosophy. According to bell hooks, "The primary contradiction in Western cultural thought is the belief that the superior should control the inferior" (*Feminist* 35). hooks believes that Western society's binaries extend from sexism to other oppressions including racism and heterosexism. Indeed, Allen remarks in her theoretical text *Off the Reservation* that European conquerors brought with them the patriarchal "father god culture" and the binaries that this culture creates (66-83). As Stephen points out in his criticism of Western philosophy, "Consciousness is the essential lie. I think therefore I am? No. You are, so you think" (4). Paralleling this challenge to philosophy is the novel's criticism of the English language itself as a dividing force:

> The language wasn't built for truth. It was a lying tongue. The only one she had. It made separations. Divided against itself. It could not allow enwholement. Only fragmentation. And it was the only language they all knew together—the people in

> her world. The tongue that only knew how to lie. The only words she had. The
> only containers for the food, the water, the soil of recovery, uncovery, discovery.
> To re learn. To re member. To put back what had been shattered. To re mind. To
> re think. The beginning so as to grasp the end. (190)

The language, the narrator notes, is a divisive force that separates and
controls its people. Similarly, Ephanie's character acts as a critique of the
Western division between body and mind; for Ephanie, memory involves not
just a psychological process, but a physical one as well. The narrator notes,
"[R]emembering rose in her body, in its muscles and in its bones" (15). In
other words, her body is a remembering force, a point which directly
confronts the Western body/mind split. As Anzaldúa argues, "The Catholic
and Protestant religions encourage fear and distrust of life and of the body;
they encourage a split between the body and the spirit and totally ignore the
soul; they encourage us to kill off parts of ourselves" (*Borderlands* 38).
Anzaldúa continues, "We are taught that the body is an ignorant animal;
intelligence dwells only in the head. But the body is smart [....] It reacts
equally viscerally to events from the imagination as it does to 'real' events"
(*Borderlands* 38). Likewise, in many of the novels in this study, including
Stigmata, Corregidora, Gulf Dreams, and *The Woman Who Owned the
Shadows*, memories are experienced physically, disproving the traditional
division between body and mind.

Allen attempts to deconstruct these binaries and to subvert Western
philosophical beliefs. *The Woman Who Owned the Shadows* does so in its
first pages, writing the story of creation from the Guadalupe perspective:

> In the beginning was the Spider. She divided the world. She made it. Thinking
> thus she made the world. She drew lines that crossed each other. Thus were the
> directions. Thus the powers. Thus were the quadrants. Thus the solstices. Thus
> were the seasons. Thus was woman [....] And the sisters awoke, those two, they
> who would give human form to the spirit which was the people. (1)

Reflecting her critique of Christianity and its system of dualities, Allen
explains in this prologue the creation story of her people. We notice that it is
the feminist creative power in Guadalupe culture that provides the world's
origins. We also notice that there are quadrants rather than eastern and
western hemispheres. This emphasis on the multiple rather than the binary is
echoed in Allen's chapter, "There's four sides to every question" (147). As
Teresa notes of her white friends, "We think in terms of black and white.
Good and bad. Cowboys and Indians. We think about things in the west like
things in the east are analyzed" (141). In other words, the everyday thinking

generated by Western philosophy presents a problem to many people, particularly because of the dualities this thinking creates. These dualities are attacked by all the authors in this study, but it is Allen's Native American culture that most emphatically challenges Western dichotomies.

Gulf Dreams and *The Woman Who Owned the Shadows* complicate the issue of bodily fragmentation and healing, for the women do not, in fact, end up together and healed. Ephanie's fall from the tree and *Gulf Dreams*'s violent fight are moments when wounds are both generated and recognized. However, the recognition does not always translate into a happy ending. The tragedy of these novels is that heteronorms drive the women away from each other. Yet empowerment and resistance come from both novels' insistence that, in Allen's words, "With each other [...] [t]hey were thus complete" (*Woman* 22). Both novels suggest that the company of women is truly the way to heal the wounds caused by the patriarchal, heteronormative demands placed on these women.

❊ CHAPTER FIVE

The Case of the Missing Women:
Chaos and the Absence of Female Bonds
in Kathy Acker's Works

> *"Friendship is always a political act, for it unites citizens*
> *into a* polis, *a (political) community" (Acker,* Bodies *104).*

> *"[P]olitics don't disappear but take place inside my body" (Acker,* Blood
> and Guts *97).*

If Emma Pérez's and Paula Gunn Allen's novels show the disintegration
of girls' and women's bonds and the consequent difficulty in healing, what,
then, does postmodern multiethnic American women's literature say about
the complete absence of female bonds? This final chapter will seek the
answer by exploring two novels by Kathy Acker, a Jewish American novelist
known for her experimental, feminist, graphically sexual and violent
aesthetic. The two novels selected for this chapter, *Blood and Guts in High
School* (1978) and *Empire of the Senseless* (1988), examine, through vastly
disjointed narrative styles, the tragically fragmented bodies of female
characters completely void of bonds to other women or girls. In both novels,
the female protagonists—both very young—lose matrilineal bonds early in
life and do not have sisters or female friends with whom to connect. "Never
having known a mother" begins Acker's *Blood and Guts* (7), and the biting
critiques of patriarchy, capitalism, and heteronormativity that follow evince
Acker's view of a world without women's community. Similarly, *Empire*
provides a character whose memory of her family—a "real" and a "fake"
mother and father, who become confused and conflated (10, 82)—becomes
skewed as the protagonist moves through a post-revolutionary time after the
Algerians have revolted against the French in 1980s Paris. The chaos, abuse,

and loss of identity suffered by both protagonists indicate Acker's scathing critiques of contemporary society, and the very absence of female bonds paradoxically insists upon feminist bonds to contest those intertwined oppressions. In other words, the destructive natures of Acker's fictional societies, which are controlled by violent, capitalist patriarchs, demand new forms of uniting and resisting.

Again, I realize that I tread dangerous ground in making these claims, and it may appear that I encourage a "traditional" nuclear family structure. Acker's novels, after all, glaringly avoid relationships such as the mother-daughter bonds of Theresa Hak Kyung Cha's *Dictée*, the community of Toni Morrison's *Beloved*, and the layered female ancestry of Phyllis Alesia Perry's *Stigmata* and Gayl Jones's *Corregidora*. Therefore, I must reiterate that a mother's presence is not necessary in order for a stable identity to be discovered. In fact, the nuclear family structure is actually the catalyst for much of the destruction in Acker's novels. Fathers exhibit violent and sexual oedipal control over their daughters, even when the mother is briefly present, as in *Empire*. Therefore, I want to suggest that Acker's work, unique in this study, emphasizes the total absence of female collectivity as the entrance point for patriarchal rule, the symbol of which is the diseased, mutilated, wounded female body. Women's bonds are effectively precluded in these settings, and recognition of shared wounds thus becomes impossible. In an environment of complete patriarchal rule, bereft of female bonds, the female body becomes a fragmentary site marked and marred by masculine dominance. Hence, even in the distorted realities that Acker creates, female community is still the primary means for contesting patriarchal power.

Acker believes that "art and the political processes of the community should be interwoven" ("Apparatus" par. 6), a stance which is evidenced in her fiction. She sees writing as a way of subverting all forms of authority: patriarchy, parental rule, heteronorms, and importantly, the authoritarian text. Her provocative and rebellious writing technique, influenced by William S. Burroughs, Gertrude Stein, and Black Mountain poetry (Wollen 4, 6, 3), is known for its appropriation and rewriting of other published texts. Acker freely borrows from other authors, or "plagiarizes," as many critics call it (Wollen 1, Dick 115, Phillips 173), and Acker herself eloquently argues that copyright should be abolished (*Bodies* 98-105). As Wollen observes, it is no coincidence that Acker often incorporates parrots and pirates into her novels, for parroting and pirating are ways of describing her use of other published texts (2). Even more striking, as Peter Wollen points out, is that Acker does not expect anyone to read any of her novels the whole way through (Wollen 1).

Her biography sheds some light on her unique and disturbing style. Born in Manhattan to a Jewish family in the 1940s, the openly bisexual Acker married and divorced twice and worked as a stripper. As a graduate student in the 1960s, Acker lived in San Diego and then San Francisco. In the 1970s, she moved to New York, where emerging avant-garde styles further influenced her work (Wollen 5). Finally, she lived in England in the mid-1980s, where she reverted to a more "narrative" style, as we see in *Empire*, which Wollen calls her "most narrative book" (10, 1). After a diagnosis of breast cancer in 1996, Acker underwent a double mastectomy. When her cancer did not disappear, Acker became disillusioned by Western medicine (a trope we recall from Cha's *Dictée*, as well) and sought alternatives until her death in 1997.

Acker's cynicism of Western culture becomes evident in her fiction. In addition to these focuses on Western society, sexuality, and gender, this chapter will complicate ethnicity, as Acker did not identify herself as a Jewish author. Therefore, the importance of ethnicity will become more ambiguous and problematic in this chapter. Though she did not identify with any specific ethnic group, her writing continually questions the role of ethnic, gender, sexual, and class identity in her characters. Much has been written on Acker's fiction, but much more needs to be said. The current scholarship focuses largely on Acker's provocative style, though a few studies address the body and families.[27] Significantly, all the scholarship on Acker's works fails to ask the question, "How would Acker's novels be different if women were not isolated from one another?" Thus, there is ample room for development, as the intersections of women's community and fragmented, mutilated, wounded, and scarred females bodies have yet to be analyzed.

Like the other novels in this study, *Blood and Guts* and *Empire* use the fragmented female body as one of their most prominent and loaded images. Acker was interested in Gilles Deleuze and Félix Guattari's theories, and we can see in her characters traces of their "becoming-woman," a concept that indicates the lack of stable identities, and interestingly, a concept which is "inseparable" from Deleuze and Guattari's "Body without Organs," a fragmentary body that is mutilated or in some way "inefficient" (276, 150). Also, as in the other novels in this study, the wounded, scarred, marked, or mutilated female body works as a criticism of patriarchy, racism, heteronormativity, and classism/capitalism. The major difference, however, between Acker's novels and the other novels in this study is that there is no female community. Therefore, there is no recognition of shared wounds through which oppression can be resisted.

In fact, the female body becomes even further fragmented as each novel progresses, with the female bodies being marked, mutilated, and wounded by men/boys. The males control the girls' movement, effectively preventing female agency. Acker's works generate striking examples of what Mary Daly might call a "sadosociety," a society informed by "sadospirituality," which "demands the destruction of women's ancestral Memory, the blocking of our capacity to conceive, speak, and act upon our own Original Words" (35-36). Unlike the novels by Morrison, Cha, Perry, and Jones, Acker's works do not have a strong presence of a mother or grandmother who generates historical memory or recognition of shared histories. Each novel does mention the mother and grandmother of the female protagonist, yet these maternal presences fade immediately within the first pages of each novel. *Blood and Guts*'s Janey Smith (a name significant for its simplicity and ordinariness) loses her mother when Janey is a year old. On the other hand, *Empire*'s Abhor (another significant name, suggesting her birth into a world she will hate, or perhaps suggesting the world's hatred of her) begins with the story of her grandmother and her mother, both of whom are now deceased. Moreover, the stories of Abhor's mother quickly become obscured, such that Abhor cannot differentiate between her "real" mother and her "fake" mother (10). In other words, matrilineal bonds are virtually nonexistent in these novels.

Even more problematic, however, is the lack of any other significant female characters whatsoever. Unlike *Gulf Dreams* and *The Woman Who Owned the Shadows*, we meet no strong female characters with whom the protagonist may potentially unite. Janey is raised by her incestuous father, and the other major characters of *Blood and Guts* are Tommy the Scorpion, President Jimmy Carter, the Persian slavetrader, and Jean Genet, all of whom use Janey for their own (generally sexual or capitalistic) pursuits. Likewise, in *Empire*, Abhor is raised by an incestuous father, and she moves through the plot with Thivai, the young male protagonist. Thivai and another man, Mark, unite to imprison and mutilate Abhor, while the remainder of the women are, according to Abhor, prostitutes with whom Abhor feels she cannot associate (109). Hence, women/girls in both novels, aside from the protagonists, are generally absent or silent. Unlike some of the other novels in this study, Acker's novels also point to the inability to find meaningful relationships with men. The female body in Acker's works is fragmented by patriarchy, heteronormativity, and capitalism, but also by specific men or boys. When the lack of female bonds precludes the ability to heal these wounds, chaos ensues. Yet this is not to say that the novels are not empowering, for Acker sees her writing as a way of subverting, challenging, and rebelling against the dominant culture; thus, her works can be seen as empowering and extraordinarily resistant texts that urge women to seek out bonds with other women.

Subversion in *Blood and Guts in High School*

When a reader first opens *Blood and Guts*, what she likely notices is the attempt, in the novel's opening pages, to unsettle the reader by bringing father and daughter together in an incestuous relationship. Ten-year-old Janey Smith, "Never having known a mother, her mother had died when Janey was a year old," depends on her father, Johnny Smith (another name significant for its ordinariness) for "everything," and his role is "boyfriend, brother, sister, money, amusement, and father" (7). "[B]oyfriend" suggests the incestuous relationship the reader will discover shortly, while "brother, sister" points to the gender play that is so prevalent in Acker's fiction. The words "money, amusement" symbolize the critique of capitalism that we will see again and again in this novel. And "father," the last of these, indicates that of all his roles, tyrannical as they may be, this man's fathering is perhaps least important to him. When they talk about their sex life, the taboo of incest is breached, and while Janey speaks like an experienced adult here, the entrance of her stuffed animal into the discussion reminds us that she is only a child: "You told me you were just friends like me and Peter (*Janey's stuffed lamb*) and you weren't going to sleep together. It's not like my sleeping around with all these art studs" (9). Sadly, we learn that Janey's young body is also ridden with sexually transmitted diseases (10). Within the novel's opening pages, then, we have already found a provocative and disturbing example of the fragmented female body—a body which seems to be at the mercy of that primary patriarchal figure; since "patriarchy" in its simplest form means "rule by the father." Hence, *Blood and Guts* provides perhaps the most literal form of patriarchy of the novels within this study.

As Janey notes in her discussion with Bill Russle, her father's best friend, "Right now we're at the edge of a new era in which, for all sorts of reasons, people will have to grapple with all sorts of difficult problems, leaving us no time for the luxury of expressing ourselves artistically" (10).

This statement implies, as Karen Brennan points out, the "demise" of "artistic expression" (258), and it suggests that Acker will take pains to express herself artistically in this novel. And in fact, *Blood and Guts* is one of the most fragmented novels in this study, using postmodern style replete with shock value, shifting settings and perspectives, graphic sexuality, and many mythical elements; these narrative choices overtly challenge the authoritarian novel and resist dominant ideologies. Hence, for Acker, like all of the other authors in this study, postmodern style is embraced as a political, feminist tool. Acker does not use postmodern style only to reveal self-reflexively the inner workings of the novel. Rather, as she notes in "Apparatus," this style is used for a more political purpose:

> I had come to the end of certain areas of what's called "Postmodernist theory." I began thinking that there is enough taking apart already. The society in which I grew up, the very hypocritical society of the 50s, is over with, and now everything is very surface, knowable. So, there's no reason to have to constantly take things apart and investigate them to see how they work. What we really need is some kind of instruction. I greatly distrust the usual bourgeois linear narrative of the nineteenth century, where the reader identifies with the character and the character goes through various moral crises. So I was searching structurally for a new kind of narrative, and that's when I became very interested in myths. Myths were narratives that were presented prior to that whole bourgeois structure. (par. 2)

Acker is thus a highly conscious writer, experimenting with a mythical postmodern style that can be seen in the plot of the novel.

In *Blood and Guts*'s dreamlike storyline, Janey becomes a sort of epic, tragic heroine. She is raised in Merida, on the Yucatan. This geographical placement is explored by Brennan, who helpfully notes that, "As 'ruin,' slowly crumbling over time, the Mayan site is also a figure for the mother's cut-up body, a figure that itself resembles Acker's pastiched text"; she continues by noting that this feminized text suggests both "the pre-Oedipal" and "the geography of a woman's body, a site that is all too often perceived by patriarchy as 'memorable' fragments" (254). Brennan appropriately connects the fragmented text to the female body in this childhood setting. Certainly, the combination of fragmented texts and fragmented bodies that we see immediately signifies a meaningful interconnection of the two.

This mythical shifting in geography continues throughout the dreamlike plot. Janey shifts identities and spaces, embodying Rosi Braidotti's "nomadic subject" whose identity is "against an essential unity" (22). Her identity is fluid and changeable, as we see from her movements. From Merida, Janey moves to New York City, where she goes to high school, drops out, and joins a gang called the Scorpions.   Unfortunately, the Scorpions are as close a community as Janey will have in her life, though their activities are anything but nurturing: "[W]e did exactly what we wanted and it was good. We got drunk. We used drugs. We fucked. We hurt each other sexually as much as we could" (32).   But even though Janey thinks this lifestyle is "good," we know from her childhood that sexuality is problematic, not empowering, for her.   As Barrett Watten aptly notes, "Sexuality is not necessarily liberation in Acker; rather, it is the energetic disturbance of a wound and an attempt to repair it" (73).   Indeed, while Janey seems to feel as though she has liberated herself from her father, her self-fragmenting behaviors exhibit her ongoing, destructive tendencies, which remain as consequences of her father's sexual abuse.

After leaving the Scorpions in 1977, Janey acquires a job at the local "hippy bakery" (37), rents a small apartment, and is soon kidnapped and sold into sex slavery under the "Persian slave trader" (65).   When Janey learns she has cancer, the slavetrader suddenly leaves. Inexplicably, Janey finds a passport and travels to Tangier, Morocco, where she meets Jean Genet in a café.   Then, Janey works in slave-like conditions in the fields south of Alexandria, and from here, she is incarcerated for stealing from Genet. Although Genet now dislikes Janey, he decides "it'll be wild" to join her in prison, so he steals, too (135).   Then, while in prison, Janey tells Genet a lengthy and likely imagined story of her affair with President Carter (119-127).   This graphic and disturbing narrative suggests how deeply entrenched in patriarchy Janey is, for even though Carter is portrayed as a disgusting and horrific being, metonymically representing "America" itself (127), Janey wants to continue her relationship with him (127).   After mysteriously escaping from prison, she and Genet travel to Cairo, Minya, Asyut, and Luxor. At the end of their travels, Genet gives her some money and leaves to see one of his plays. When he departs, Janey abruptly dies. Yet the novel does not end here. Instead, it continues with a section called "The World," a series of poems and drawings.[28]   This ending section challenges the authoritarian, objective text, for the death of the protagonist usually culminates in the end of a novel. The suggestion is that Janey is a victim of a world in which she has no control, and that this world will continue without her.

Within this extremely fluid, dreamlike, plot, the writing itself is drastically and almost incomprehensibly fragmented. Early in the novel, there is a repetition of the same lines:

A few hours later they woke up together and decided they would spend the whole day together since it was their last day. Janey would meet Johnny at the hotel where he worked when he got off from work.

They ate raw fish salad (*cerviche*) at a Lebanese joint and tea at a Northern Chinese place. They held hands. They didn't talk about Sally or anything heavy.

Johnny left her, telling her he'd be home later. (21-25)

These lines are repeated six times, a narrative strategy that is usually intended to show special emphasis. However, the repetition of these mundane lines, with different text between each occurrence, implies that this final day is occurring over and over, which confuses rather than emphasizes their meaning.

Moreover, a first-time reader might approach the opening twelve pages of *Blood and Guts* by thinking she is reading a drama, for these pages are written as dramatic dialogue. Interestingly, this opening drama between Janey and her father sets up Acker's critique of patriarchy, for Janey's dialogue presents her as a stereotypical, jealous lover: "I get hysterical when I don't understand" (12). The dialogue emphasizes the jealousy and rivalry instilled in women in patriarchal society, such that they feel they must compete with one another for male approval. Janey is jealous and hateful of Sally both for her beauty and for her stealing Janey's lover/father. Thus, the novel suggests right away, through convoluted narrative, blatant sexuality, and offensive stereotypes, that the traditional authoritarian text, and the patriarchal connotations that go with it, are in jeopardy.

The Fragmented Female Body
in *Blood and Guts in High School*

The fragmented text emphasizes the symbolically fragmented body, and in some cases, the text even *shows* the fragmented body. Hence, text is used to mirror the state of the female body and to offer a critique of the oppressions that generate these fragmentations. The first noticeable use of fragmentation is, in fact, on the covers of both novels. Each entails a photograph of Acker herself, with large fractures or tears drawn across the photographs; in other words, Acker's concern with the fragmented female body is evident before we even open her book. Acker notes that this overarching interest in the body comes from a socially repressed, "hypocritical" society: "I grew up in a society where the body was excluded, and in a very major way women's bodies were and are excluded from the society" ("Apparatus," par. 22). Perhaps for this reason, Acker's task seems to be releasing the body from any societal constraints and taboos.

Likewise, the title of *Blood and Guts in High School* indicates that Acker will take the body at its most basic level—that of the tissues that compose it—and connect it to its social environment. In other words, the novel will explore the social construction of the body. Interestingly, the title suggests that this social environment is high school, yet, ironically, none of the novel is actually set in a high school. In fact, Janey drops out of school at age thirteen. The title does, however, serve as a reminder that the character we are observing is quite young. It also suggests that the social atmosphere of the pubescent age group is significant—part-time jobs, experimentation with sex and drugs, early gang membership—all are part of the social milieu that Acker tackles in *Blood and Guts*. The phrase "blood and guts" is used three times in the novel, with the final time in the closing poem: "Blood and guts in high school / This is all I know / Parents teachers boyfriends / All have got to go" (165). The repetition of the title three times in the novel suggests Acker's focus on the fundamental, biological construction of the body in relation to the social construction of the gendered body.

This construction begins with the oedipal, father-daughter relationship between Janey and Johnny. Their relationship suggests the power dynamics that will characterize all of Janey's heterosexual relationships in the novel. Hence, Acker successfully problematizes all heterosexual relationships as perverse. For example, Janey also has sexual relationships with Mr. Linker, the Persian slave trader who imprisons, beats, and rapes Janey. Regardless, she comes to "love" Mr. Linker. Likewise, Janey becomes involved in a sexual relationship, likely imaginary, with President Carter, who, of course, symbolizes the entire patriarchal hegemony upon which the United States is built. It is significant that Janey believes she has sex with the President, for her involvement with the United States' highest symbol of authority and status indicates how fully immersed she is in patriarchal hegemony; she has invoked the offensive, antifeminist epithet of "sleeping her way to the top," and she is still horribly oppressed and fragmented. Janey's perverse relationships with each of these men portray Acker's harsh criticism of patriarchy and heteronormativity, and they force the reader to confront the power dynamics of all relationships.

To further her reading of the fragmented body, Acker makes use of many sketches within the first half of the novel, each of which involves a nude figure. The nude sketches challenge readers' underlying assumptions in two ways: First, they interrupt reader expectations, and second, they call attention to Western art, which tends to objectify the female figure. There are nine images, four of which are of women or female parts (19, 22, 62, 63), and six of which are of men or male parts (8, 14, 22, 24, 27, 30). (One image has both a male and female figure [22].) The heavier focus on the male subject suggests a criticism of the larger presence of the female nude in art. The images of male subjects include headless torsos and male reproductive organs, and these fragmented male images may suggest that Acker is concerned with the fragmented male body as much as she is with the female body. However, it is significant to note that the only figure with a head is a female image, and this woman is the one in the only heterosexual sketch. (The other sketches depict just one gender in each.) Therefore, Acker is perhaps suggesting that women are expected to be most complete when they are with men or involved in heterosexual relationships; hence, the only woman with a head is also the only woman with a man. In other words, Acker criticizes a society that recognizes women as whole only when they participate in heteronormative structures.

One of the most interesting images is the sketch captioned "Ode to a Grecian Urn" (63). This image entails a female body (again, headless) tied at the wrists and ankles. The body is positioned with arms stretched upwards, such that the woman's symmetry and lines resemble the shape of an urn. The caption repeats what Mr. Linker, the Iranian slave trader, has said: "All of our culture comes from ancient Greece" (61). The image, therefore, reminds us that much Western art paints women as sexual and visual commodities. Moreover, this sketch suggests the novel's criticism of Western philosophy as a confining (hence the bound wrists and ankles) and gendered ideology. Parallel to this image, Janey's body becomes the means through which critiques of dominant ideologies are enacted. She notes early on that her body is riddled with sexually-transmitted diseases. We can safely assume, in fact, that the cancer Janey acquires and dies from (at an extremely early age) is a product of a sexually transmitted virus. One sketch shows Janey's enflamed vagina with the caption, "My cunt red ugh" (19). Along the same lines, Janey labels herself as "tough, rotted, putrid beef" (18). Hence, like the sketches of diseased, decapitated, and fragmented female bodies, Janey sees herself as a mutilated and diseased body.

The abuse, disease, and victimization Janey suffers as a child lead her into drastically destructive sadomasochistic tendencies and further victimization. Janey leaves her job at the bakery because "[i]t's hard to get beyond sex" (42), and she wants to spend all her time with her lover from the

Scorpion gang, Tommy. Together, they "[a]ttacked strangers with broken bottles. Hit people over the head with hard objects. Kicked the guts out of people on the streets. Started fights and riots" (42). When all Janey's Scorpion friends are anticlimactically killed in a police-chase, Janey, now thirteen and without the only community she will ever know, leaves high school and moves to an East Village slum where she lives in a tiny apartment. During this period, she has an affair with an eighty-year-old man, and she describes the self-fragmentary, violent behaviors in which she engages: "He took a heavy leather belt and whipped me across the back as he fucked me [....] It hurt almost too much and I liked it" (59). However, Janey soon realizes that this self-destructive behavior is emotionally and physically damaging: "I've been so repressed in this crummy room like a prison every day doing less and less and thinking more and more until something's gonna break probably my body" (59). And sure enough, Janey's body is "broken" when her apartment is broken into; two men enter, and Janey is beaten, kidnapped, and sold into sex slavery. The men who kidnap Janey tell her, "First we'll train you, then we'll sell you" (61). Janey, abused first by her father and then by Tommy and the eighty-year-old man, has now become a sexual commodity whose body will be further tortured and diseased in the brothel into which she is sold.

The opening passages of incest, the sketches of fragmentary bodies, and the sadomasochistic relationships in which Janey engages all point to the larger critique of fragmentation that the novel offers. While *Blood and Guts* is often difficult to comprehend, it offers valuable criticisms of the state of the female body. Even in moments when Janey feels liberated—when she travels or joins the Scorpions, for example—she is consistently confined by patriarchal structures. She in essence moves from one prison to another: from her abusive father's house to the capitalist bakery to the Scorpions and Tommy to a miniature apartment to a field of slaves to an actual prison. As Janey's book report notes, "We all live in prison. Most of us don't know we live in prison" (65). The idea is that all of Janey's movements are controlled by men whose only motive is maintaining power. The series of movements culminates in Janey's abrupt death alone in Luxor. Her diseased and now deceased body shores up the novel's insistence that patriarchal hegemonies in all forms must be contested. The means to do so in this novel is clearly missing, for the glaring omission in all of Janey's travels and relationships is any bond whatsoever with another female character.

Confusion in *Empire of the Senseless*

Unlike the other novels in this study, *Blood and Guts* does not have a dedication, and the dedications, as we have noticed, often emphasize the key connections between mothers and daughters, or between women. On the other hand, *Empire* is dedicated "to my tattooist." The lack of dedication to family or female relatives and friends, as well as the dedication to Acker's tattooist, reifies Acker's commitment to examining the body and the absence of female bonds. *Empire* begins with a young girl, Abhor, a cyborg who is "part robot, part black" (3), telling the story of her grandmother and her grandmother's family, a "German-Jewish family which was real wealthy" (3). The grandmother, Nana, raises Abhor's father but does not educate him. Abhor's father, in turn, raises Abhor in his footsteps, and she is taught very little. Significantly, one of her only lessons from her father, which will be explained shortly, is how to mutilate her own body. Moreover, Abhor's father, like Janey Smith's father, engages in an incestuous relationship with his daughter. Likewise, this novel includes a few sketches, though they are far fewer and are not sexually graphic, like those in *Blood and Guts*. Rather, they are images of the tattoos described in the novel. Also like *Blood and Guts*, *Empire* is highly fragmented. Thus, *Empire* entails many of the same concerns as does *Blood and Guts*. *Empire*, however, tells the stories of two characters, Abhor, the black female cyborg, and Thivai, an adolescent male. As the novel shifts perspectives, times, and places in a dreamlike way similar to *Blood and Guts*, the reader follows the story of a Parisian setting in which the Algerians have revolted. Much of the plot is nearly impossible to follow, thus subverting further the genre of the novel. Acker explains her rationale for subverting the linear, cohesive novel:

> In a bourgeois narrative the text is supposedly a mirror of that which is outside the text, so the reason that you identify with the character is that you believe the character goes in this mirror version of your life, and comes out with some bit of knowledge. This idea, which is basically impossible after Roland Barthes, is that you can know, that you can read a text, that you can learn something, that you can in a way possess knowledge: you are a centralized identity, and you as this centralized "I" are capable of knowing it. I mean it's based on Descartes. I don't live in that kind of world, so I would never go to a piece of art thinking that I can get a moral message from it, and that I'm in that much control. I think the real relations are very different. ("Apparatus" par. 8)

In this conversation, Acker notes that her novels are not meant to teach any sort of lesson or moral and that she rejects the Cartesian notion of the unified subject, concepts that we will see throughout these two novels. Thus, *Empire* seeks to critique patriarchy through subversion of the conventional novel.

Family and the Fragmented Female Body in *Empire of the Senseless*

While Janey Smith's family history is described only briefly in a dramatic conversation, and we receive only the present-day actions of Janey's and Johnny's interactions, Abhor's family history is described in detail in *Empire*. The first section, according to Acker's "A Few Notes on Two of My Books," portrays a "society which is defined by the oedipal taboo," which she defines as "phallic centricity and total domination on the political, economic, social, and personal levels" (35). Accordingly, the first title in this section is "Rape by the Father." We learn that Abhor is a female cyborg, "part robot, and part black"—the robot heritage is never explained—and in the first subheading, we learn about "My Grandmother" (*Empire* 3). Abhor's paternal grandmother was born to a wealthy German-Jewish family who left Germany and went to Paris when nationalistic social influences began to generate the Nazis (3). Nana is prostituted at the age of ten, "the right age," by her parents when they arrive in Paris (3). Ten, we recall, is the age of Janey in *Blood and Guts*; Acker apparently sees this age as the time when childhood innocence and prepubescent curiosity and vulnerability combine to make a girl easily exploitable.

As with several novels in this study, particularly Jones's *Corregidora* and Perry's *Stigmata*, Abhor feels an attachment to her grandmother. She first notes, "As my grandmother got older, she got more stubborn and determined. I'm stubborn and determined" (3-4), indicating her inheritance of her grandmother's traits. After Nana's young lover, Alexander, is executed by the Parisian Vice-Squad (6), Nana marries a wealthy man (7), for as Abhor notes, "The poor can reply to the crime of society, to their economic deprivation retardation primitivism lunacy boredom hopelessness, only by collective crime or war. One form collective crime takes is marriage" (7). However, Abhor notes that "because I perceived what marriage was for my grandmother and because I love her, I am not able to sexually love another human being or accept another human being's love" (7). She continues, "If I have to love, out of desperation or desperately, I know love only when it's allied with hate" (7). This statement subtly connects Abhor to her grandmother and suggests that, like Ursa Corregidora's grandmother and great-grandmother, Nana and her experiences largely shape Abhor's relationships with men. Of course, this lineage is not foregrounded, as is Ursa's, nor is it fully coherent, for we recall that Abhor is Jewish, part black, and (inexplicably) part robot. Moreover, Nana dies long before Abhor knows her. Hence, Acker has effectively complicated the role of matrilineage in this novel, showing that the female protagonist is truly without any cohesive bonds with other women and girls.

In the next section, simply entitled "Daddy," we learn more about Abhor's father, Bud, who becomes the embodiment of Acker's intersecting critiques of patriarchy and capitalism: "Daddy was Nana's only kid. She adored him. She gave him everything she could. He, in turn, turned to her as a mother turns to her child. They formed a closed world" (8). Nana, however, fails to educate Abhor's father: "Since he had turned to grandma rather than outward to the world, he had no morals, for any morality presumes a society. [...S]he saw no reason to teach him anything or that he should learn anything" (8). It is said that Bud charms his parents and his teacher with "his complete lack of social awareness and of education. Politics, for my father, was, always, a hole" (8). Then, as Bud enters late childhood, he is orphaned: "When he was ten years old and unlearned, my grandfather, who everyone considered a saint, and Nana together killed themselves: they couldn't live without each other" (8). Therefore, Bud inherits six million dollars. For Abhor's father, money and sex become intertwined because, as Abhor notes, "from the night he lost his virginity, daddy never had trouble finding lovers. Lovers were men and women to whom he gave gifts, not love or need" (8-9). At the age of forty, Abhor's father gets married "because he wanted to propagate himself once" (9). His fifteen-year-old wife marries him because, as Abhor notes, "Sex was joined to money" (9). Hence, we see a layered critique of marriage, with Abhor's parents and grandparents engaging in relationships largely driven by social pressures and money.

Because Bud married only to have a child, Abhor understands that she belongs to him: "By him. His" (9). And even though he himself is uneducated, "He educated me. I was educated the way he had been educated" (9). Therefore, Abhor says, "I don't know anything about politics and I never read newspapers. As a result of this education I just like trouble" (9). Abhor is raised by an ignorant and, as we find out shortly, abusive father. Sadly, unlike the other protagonists in this study, Abhor cannot turn to her mother, for her mother "hated me" (9). Moreover, we are never sure who Abhor's true mother is, for Bud tells Abhor that her real mother abandoned her at the hospital. Bud's young wife, then, becomes "my mother who was now fake" (10). In other words, Abhor's female connections are distorted, absent, or ruptured to the point that she seems to have no female lineage whatsoever. Inevitably, the only female connection she now has, Abhor's "fake mother," commits suicide, leaving Abhor with no female connections. (A mysterious younger sister, Audry, is mentioned late in the novel, but she seems never to have come into contact with Abhor [90, 109].) Abhor's lack of female bonds and her dependence on her power-hungry, incestuous father set her up—much like Janey Smith in *Blood and Guts*—for relationships that perpetuate this hierarchy.

In her concise observation, Nicole Cooley argues that for Acker, "the body is always a text" (193), and in *Empire*, as in *Blood and Guts*, we see the body as a text inscribed with horrific oppressions. Abhor is physically fragmented by her father early on, both sexually and through self-mutilation. What begins as a seemingly caring relationship quickly deteriorates into a disturbing and violent scene:

> Daddy played all sorts of games with me. He taught me how to throw a real football. He taught me gymnastics. He trained me into total physical perfection.

> Then he taught me a final trick. He showed me how to insert a razor blade into my wrist just for fun. Not for any other reason. Thus, I learned how to approach and understand nature, how to make gargantuan red flowers, like roses, blooming, drops of blood, so full and dripping the earth under them, my body, shook for hours afterwards. During those afterhours, I fantasized my blood pouring outwards. This was relief that there were no decisions left. (9-10)

In essence, Abhor learns to accept fragmentation as part of her existence. Because her father, her only family, takes away her "decisions" and imposes this early mutilation on her, a fragmented existence seems natural to Abhor. Moreover, Bud soon turns his daughter into his sex slave. When Bud finds out that Abhor, now fourteen, has had sex with a young man, he jealously locks her up (11), tells his community that Abhor is "a cripple" (14), and convinces her mother that he "was saving me from marriage because marriage is the worst life any woman can have," to which "[m]y mother agreed" (14). Thus, Abhor is locked away and kept as a sexual object for her incestuous father. While Bud eventually disappears at sea (19), his fragmenting actions are still reflected in Abhor's nightmares when we meet her as an older child:

Daddy. Pull off my fingernails. My back has been carved into roses. You scream that it's not only by you. As if you're alive or as if I'm not dreaming. As if I really possessed you and you really possessed me, we tore off each other's head and ate out the contents, then pecked out the remaining eyes, pulled out the sharks' teeth and sucked opium out of the gums, my vagina was bleeding. (84)

The dreamed father's comment that fragmentation is "not only by" him is significant, for he rightly suggests that the oppressions Abhor will face are systemic.

Like *Blood and Guts*, Acker's *Empire* places great emphasis on the writing of the body, particularly the female body. Also, like *Blood and Guts*, overt sexuality and violence characterize this novel. The two main characters meet when Abhor comes to Thivai with a mission from her boss—she and Thivai must find a "construct" named Kathy (34). Why Acker inserts her own name here is arguable, but what is interesting is that this supposed catalyst for the novel's action never actually comes to fruition. In fact, the "construct" is not mentioned again after this meeting scene. Instead, Abhor's cyborg body is described in detail from Thivai's point of view:

A transparent cast ran from her knee to a few millimetres below her crotch, the skin mottled by blue purple and green patches which looked like bruises but weren't. Black spots on the nails, finger and toe, shaded into gold. Eight derms, each a different colour size and form, ran in a neat line down her right wrist and down the vein of the right upper thigh. A transdermal unit, separated from her body, connected to the input trodes under the cast by means of thin red leads. A construct. (33-34)

Abhor's fragmented body, half human and half robot, is significant, for as Abhor notes, "Mentality is the mirror of physicality. The body is a mirror of the mind" (65). This point suggests that a fragmented body such as Abhor's reflects a fragmented identity, and it recalls Maurice Merleau-Ponty's observation that one cannot exist without the other (39). Of course, Abhor's mental state is quite confused and disconnected. Abhor is unsure of whether her parents are real or fake, and her retelling of her rape later in the novel is different from the first telling of it in the novel's opening pages. As she concedes, "[M]y memory's always been poor" (66). Thus, we have an unreliable narrator; we receive only fragmentary bits of memory from Abhor, and what we do learn is always uncertain. What we do know, however, is that Abhor's sexuality is a disjointed and painful element of her identity: "[I]t seemed to me that my sexuality was a source of pain. That my sexuality was the crossroads not only of my mind and body but of my life and death.

My sexuality was ecstasy" (65). In sexuality, Abhor finds that body and mind are inseparable, and because her sexuality is both "ecstasy" and "pain," we learn that the disjointed nature of her mind and body is a repercussion of her father's control.

In a layered understanding of bodily marking, the novel also uses tattooing, of which Acker herself is quite fond. Despite Arthur F. Redding's belief that *Empire*'s tattoos show "the subordination of the masochistic subject via a ritual scarification" (290), Acker herself believes that tattoos are a way not of fragmenting the body, but of making the body more complete. Regarding tattooing, Acker says some revealing things that should be quoted at length:

> When you're dealing with tattooing, you're remaking the body. On the other hand, you're going in and listening to the body, and it's not so much remaking the body as it is finding out about the body, finding out what's there, and the two processes come together in the same process called tattooing. If some tattooist just goes in and does whatever, it's not going to work. Ed Hardy [Acker's tattoo artist, to whom *Empire* is dedicated] is one of the best tattooists in the world and the way Ed works is to really get interested in the person, to ask a lot of questions, to try to find out what they're about. A good part of the body is the imaginary. He tries to find out what the body looks like as a whole, how's the whole tattoo going to fit into the body as a whole. He's in there trying to learn about the body. The process of tattooing for him is learning about someone's body, which is learning about someone. He's not going in there to re-make the body in terms of some model that's outside that body. ("Apparatus" par. 20)

What is so interesting in Acker's discussion is the note that what is portrayed on the outside of the body is a reflection of some inner "being." Hence, Abhor's note that "being" includes mentality, physicality, and feeling (133) is, in fact, Acker's own perspective. Likewise, Abhor's statement that the body mirrors the mind (65) exemplifies the tattoo artist's perspective, for he believes that he must locate some inner essence and reproduce it on the outside of the body. Interestingly, *Empire* experiments with its own form of tattooing, which is described carefully: "This new way of tattooing consisted of raising defined parts of the flesh up with a knife. The tattooer then draws a string through the raised points of flesh. Various coloration methods can be used on the living points" (134). This new mode of tattooing devised by Acker furthers her conviction that there is some inner image or sense of wholeness that can be inscribed on the flesh, and that there are various ways of doing so.

Tattooing is not, Acker notes, a mode of control: "I don't 'have' a text outside of the body that I want to impose on the body in some kind of fascistic way" ("Apparatus" par. 22). The fact that Acker grew up in the 1950s begs Acker's poignant question, "So why is the body central?" She answers, "Because our bodies have been denied, because maybe Gloria Steinem is allowed to say that we should be equal to men, but when it comes to menstruation it's 'hide that dirty pad!'" ("Apparatus" par. 22). Acker's belief in the centrality of the body is emphasized in her celebration of tattooing. Acker's praise of elective tattooing as a subversive and empowering strategy is explained when she notes in *Empire* that tattooing has, historically, been imposed as a means of control: "Cruel Romans had used tattoos to mark and identify mercenaries, slaves, criminals, and heretics" (130). This point connects with Carol E. Henderson's argument that enslaved persons were marked in order to make visible those "rebellious" slaves. Thivai, likewise, describes the stigma that comes with being tattooed: "Between one-third and two-thirds of all prison inmates wear tattoos. Being tattooed shows a tendency for violence, property crime, and self-destruction or self-mutilation. There is a strong relationship between tattooing and the commission of violent, assaultive acts" (148). In other words, prison inmates and other criminals are marked, as Henderson would point out, like slaves who evince a "dangerous" tendency. Acker's *Empire*, however, points to the argument I have made throughout this study. These forced tattoos, or bodily marks, represent some form of historical oppression. However, it is in the recognition of shared wounds that people find community, heal wounds, and resist oppression. As Abhor notes, "Among the early Christians, tattoos, stigmata indicating exile, which at first had been forced upon their flesh, finally actually served to enforce their group solidarity" (130). Likewise, Acker herself subverts the practice of tattooing by claiming it as a resistant, feminist strategy.

In contrast to tattooing as a subversive strategy, the novel clearly portrays bodily fragmentation as a symbol of patriarchy. This use of fragmentation is especially evident when Abhor is imprisoned (again paralleling Janey Smith), and Thivai and his new companion, Mark, attempt to help her escape. The men insist that she must seriously injure herself in the process in order to be more "heroic": "We told her that [escaping] was too easy. She was going to have to get permanently and seriously maimed escaping from her jail because escaping from jail is a difficult and dangerous thing for a man to do" (202). When Abhor responds, "But I'm not a man," Mark replies, "Then you're not going to get out of jail" (202). Mark matter-of-factly explains, "A man has to endure pain and more severe tribulations to show that he has the power to make someone of himself. Being maimed is the way a man shows he's a man" (202). What is so interesting in this scene is that it is men who are encouraging Abhor, a young woman, to mutilate herself.

Moreover, while Abhor is in prison, Thivai decides she should write some prison memoirs. However, he must teach her to write; according to Thivai, "Abhor didn't know how to write because, being black, she was uneducated" (201). Thivai takes control of Abhor's fate and determines that they will "make Abhor, though she was uneducated, into a great writer so that she'ld [sic] have a reason for being in jail for the rest of her life. And at that time, society needed a great woman writer" (203). Interestingly, Thivai's method of teaching Abhor to write involves physically and painfully fragmenting her body. During their first lesson, he begins to mutilate her on his own terms:

> First we taught her how to slice up her thumb with a penknife blade. That way she'ld have a lot of blood.
>
> Abhor didn't want to do that cause she was a big scaredy-cat. I told her good that if she wanted to be great, as great as a man, she'ld have to learn how to endure tribulations even more severe than pain and still keep her mouth shut [....]
>
> Mark didn't listen to her palavering, but held her right thumb right down, and I sliced into it. We held her right thumb down cause Abhor wrote with her right hand. Writers need disability or madness they can overcome in order to write [....] We sliced into Abhor's thumb and got some blood. (203)

Then, during their second lesson, which, chronologically, follows immediately the first lesson, Thivai notes, "To write is to reveal a heart's identity," and then "I cut into Abhor's four fingers with another penknife. There was blood all over the place" (204). As Thivai tellingly notes, "Making Abhor into a great woman writer obviously was going to take more blood than sweat" (205). In other words, writing is equated with white male territory. For black women—and the novels by Morrison, Perry and Jones would agree—writing involves blood and pain; of course, this blood and pain is often figurative and psychological. When Mark and Thivai cut Abhor despite her resistance, they literalize the process of writing characterized by many writers. Moreover, they give a very literal example of female bodily fragmentation as perpetuated by patriarchy.

The Necessity of Female Bonds

Both *Blood and Guts* and *Empire* exemplify what the other novels in this study have shown—that without women's bonds of some sort, whether matrilineal, sisterly, or romantic, patriarchal power structures will continue to be constructed and maintained. The most glaring difference between Acker's novels and the other novels in this study is that Abhor and Janey have no relationships with other women or girls whatsoever. Their familial connections are severed, and they do not have lovers, friends, or relatives with whom to unify and resist. This female absence results in chaos, loss, and fragmentation. In *Blood and Guts*, Janey must struggle to find agency in a world where she seems always to be confined. Because she loses her mother and is violated by her father, she moves from one patriarchal prison to another. She does not find any female companions after leaving her father's house, but instead finds herself in a series of violent and disturbing relationships. Johnny, Tommy, Mr. Linker, President Carter, and the other men in the novel exemplify *Blood and Guts*'s powerful call for resistance. The glaring absence of female bonds in the novel, of course, suggests that it is female bonds that could reverse some of these patriarchal power structures.

As Abhor notes, when she talks to men, she feels as though "I'm taking layers of my own epidermis, which are layers of still freshly bloody scar tissue, black brown and red, and tearing each one of them off so more and more of my blood shoots into your face" (210). This gruesome image "is what writing is to me a woman" (210). One reason for the absence of strong female characters in *Empire* is that all the women in this setting are prostitutes, and Abhor does not fit in: "In this city, women are just what they always were, prostitutes" (109). Thus, even though the women largely live in a community—"They live together and do whatever they want to do"— Abhor feels "like a mutant" as a non-prostitute because "sexuality was too devastating to me" (109). According to Abhor, prostitutes do not own cars, because all the jobs and cars belong to men; this fact means that it was "almost only women in the visible world" (110), yet these visible women are not women with whom Abhor is able to connect.

Abhor suffers a loss of identity without ties to other humans, particularly women. Even her male friend, Thivai, "was gone" (110), and Abhor "wondered what it was to have a friend. A friend who didn't go away" (110). She lays out the point this study has made throughout: "It seemed to me that human identity had to begin with and in friendship" (110). And friendship, according to Acker, can provide political power: "Friendship is always a political act, for it unites citizens into a polis, a (political) community" (*Bodies* 104). The lack of community points to Abhor's loss of identity, for as she notes, "I've never been able to or interested in recognizing myself" (111), and she notes, "I wasn't anyone" (110). Significantly, Abhor realizes that female companions could change her situation. When Abhor has the chance to ask a question to an old female fortuneteller, she asks about the possibility of female companionship:

> Was it possible that someday—someday—I would hold naked in my arms, and continue to hold and continue to hold, pressed close to my body, a woman on whose femininity and masculine strength I could lean, trusting, whose mettle and daring would place her so high in my esteem that I would long to throw myself at her feet and do as she wished? (116)

In this rare moment of openness, Abhor admits that female companionship is her one true desire. While Abhor does not find this companionship, she does discover some agency. In the end of the novels, Janey dies, but Abhor attempts to escape. Acker herself had developed a motorcycle fetish, and Abhor, rather than remaining involved with Thivai after he slices her hands, discovers a motorcycle and tries to create her own movement. This push for autonomy is extremely valuable, as it is through the motorcycle that Abhor discovers her own agency and mobility. This movement, though it is one way of contesting patriarchal constraints, does not overturn the patriarchal rule; Abhor decides she does not want to be part of the motorcycle gang, so she is now "making up the rules" (222). The novel leaves Abhor in the sunlight, thinking that some day, there might be "a human society in a world which is beautiful, a society which wasn't just disgust" (227). The implication here is that, while this harmonious world does not exist, the potential for it does.

The Question of Ethnicity in Acker's Novels

Unlike the other authors this study, Acker does not foreground her own ethnic heritage in her novels. We have seen Perry, Morrison, and Jones reaching through generations of enslaved women, Allen tackling twentieth-century Native American life, Cha addressing colonialism in Korea, and Pérez taking on the homophobia in her Chicano/a community. But Acker does not seem to write from a "Jewish" perspective, if such a perspective could be delineated. Yet even if Acker does not create Jewish characters or communities, her attention to ethnicity is evidenced throughout her work. Specifically, Acker attacks racism as a partner to capitalism and sexism. She is particularly attentive to racism against African American and Jewish characters. Dean Franco's study provides some insight on the distinction I make here. Franco notes that many authors of Jewish heritage hesitate to offer their ethnicity as a defining characteristic since "Jewishness" is not always a visible marker, as are the markers of other ethnic groups. As Franco confirms, "The alliance of African American, Chicano, Native American, and Asian American studies with postcolonial studies, materialist, and nationalist-oriented theory" demonstrates "the vast gap between how white ethnics and ethnics of color figure the place of ethnicity and cultural difference in American writing" (16). In other words, as a "white ethnic," Acker writes from a position that is not entirely "other."

While Jewish American literature is a vital component of multiethnic literature, we notice that the Jewish American author is considered somehow "less ethnic" than the African American, Asian American, Native American, or Chicana author. Franco's helpful explanation will be summarized briefly here. First, the definition of ethnicity, as Franco employs it, should be noted: "Ethnicity—cultural difference, not only indicates a minority group, but interpellates a dominant other, a dialectic where neither position is stable but always shifting in response to the gaze of the other" (103). Franco historicizes this interpellation by arguing that the United States changes its understanding of race in order to maintain a dominant white class (21). Thus, Jewish Americans have become largely assimilated into the dominant white culture. Franco notes that this assimilation is present within the literary establishment, as Jewish authors "are recipients of major national and international literary prizes, and have access to elite publication venues," while Chicano writers "write from the margins of the literary establishment" (23). Therefore, while many Chicano writers "rebel against prevailing aesthetic and ideological norms," Jewish writers "all but comprise the establishment and have been on the vanguard of literary trends throughout the century, from Henry Roth's modernism to Philip Roth's postmodernism" (23). Jewish American authors, Franco believes, are not marginalized as are other ethnic groups.

Franco's analysis is helpful in my multiethnic context, though I diverge from him on other points. As Franco notes provocatively, "Chicano writers have helped form the very language of counterhegemonic cultural criticism, while Jewish writers and critics have been comparatively absent from multicultural critical dialogues" (23). Here, I disagree with Franco, and not only because Acker is not part of his analysis. Certainly, Acker's work forms a critical, counterhegemonic, multicultural dialogue. While her Jewish heritage is not entirely visible in her writing, she nonetheless makes ethnic and racial concerns a priority, and further, she implicates capitalism and patriarchy in the problem of ongoing racism. Moreover, Acker certainly does not "comprise the establishment," as Franco would claim (23), but rather, she attacks every element of it.

Surprisingly, very few critics deal with ethnicity in Acker's works. An important reading comes from Jon Stratton, who provides an intriguing discussion of ethnicity in *Empire*. Stratton argues that the novel is, "in part, but crucially, a Jewish text" (80). He finds that the novel uses graphic violence in order to move into an era that is "post-Holocaust," believing that *Empire* provides "a pretext for a meditation on the problem of representability, in particular in relation to the Holocaust" (80). This invisible but present reference to the Holocaust, Stratton believes, is found in "the sense of a loss of moral bearings in the book"; he finds that the "sexual violation, incest, torture, violence, murder in *Empire*" suggests "a loss of moral premises, a loss also implied in the post-Holocaust recognition of the consequences for an accepted, shared morality of the Nazi decision that European Jewry had to be destroyed" (90-91). While Stratton's argument is important (and is in fact, one of the only discussions of ethnicity and the Holocaust in Acker's works), I believe that the complication of ethnicity goes even further.

Acker prioritizes ethnic and racial concerns in a daring way. Although we are never told what Janey's ethnic heritage is, she is called a "Jew" in numerous places in *Blood and Guts* (20, 130). But while we may interpret that Janey is of Jewish heritage, this information has little impact on the narrative. Rather, Acker uses characters' heritage to note her own awareness of ongoing racism, a point which is emphasized further in *Empire*. As "An Arab female" notes, in Harlem "the black hates the Jew. (And for good reason—the Jew owns black property)," and "the black hates the Arab cause Arabs started the black slave trade" (164). On top of the internal racism of Harlem, however, the whole community is a "[f]estival of police clubs" (164) in which all ethnic minorities are targeted.

By playing with ethnicity and stereotypes, Acker further critiques the role of race and ethnicity. Thivai complicates the role of ethnicity when he describes his own interplanetary ethnic heritage: "My father, I remembered, came from Alpha-Centauri [....] Unlike him, my mother, a moon-child, was just a good-for-nothing [....] I came out of a cross-racial union. Multi-racial marriages usually lead to disaster" (154). Then, when he turns eight years old, his mother "told me that my real father wasn't Alpha-Centaurian, but robotic" (155). Like Abhor, Thivai has a drastically mixed background, and by using robots and planets as ethnicities, Acker cleverly plays with stereotypes. Moreover, she connects racist, sexist, and heterosexist epithets, generating layered stereotypes that become absurd in their complexity: "My mom, cause she had been part Jewish, and cause I wasn't a girl so I couldn't marry a rich man, had wanted me to be a doctor" (186). Thivai suggests that money is important to the Jewish man and woman, and because he is a male, the best way to acquire money is to become a doctor. The clause, "cause she had been part Jewish," matter-of-factly emphasizes the stereotype of Jewish greed as if it is an understood fact of life. Acker combines several hasty generalizations into one line, generating a sarcastic criticism of stereotypes.

Empire's critique of racialized systems of oppression does not stop with this discussion of heritage. Abhor, the female protagonist, is "part robot, and part black" (3). The role of African American racism within Harlem has been noted above, but this critique is furthered when Abhor describes the racial turmoil in the world in which she and Thivai live. The Algerians have revolted, and systems of oppression that dictate the movement of specific people are installed. These systems are reminiscent of those used during American slavery or under current fascist regimes, delineating where and when groups of persons may move:

> As a result of this *urban* rather than *political* situation, by 1985 city ordinances prohibited all blacks from going anywhere at night unless accompanied by a white and carrying a special governmental ordinance. Even in broad daylight three or more blacks who talked together or even stood together without at least an equal number of whites were considered to be a terrorist cadre and subject to penal disciplines up to death. (76)

Acker is clearly fictionalizing the real governments that have regulated the movement of those seen as threats to the dominant culture or ideology. Hence, while Acker downplays her own ethnicity, her writing loudly and clearly criticizes the racism that still exists.

Challenging Western Philosophy in Acker's Novels

Of course, with Acker, many social oppressions work hand in hand with other forms of social oppression. Therefore, the regulation of movement described above is tied to the oppression that arises from capitalism as well as Western philosophy and the privileging of that which is associated with the phallus or *logos* (Derrida 81). While working as a slave on the plantation, Janey lashes out at the male boss and a male slave: "For 2,000 years you've had the nerve to tell women who we are. We use your words; we eat your food. Every way we get money has to be a crime. We are plagiarists, liars, and criminals" (132). Janey makes the radical statement that women are subordinate to men in every way. The novel seems to be a rejection of the use of man-made language and forms of expression, even though Acker is known for appropriating (and subverting) others' texts. When Janey relegates women's position to plagiarism, the reader must ask why Acker herself freely uses appropriation as a narrative style.[29] In fact, Acker uses plagiarism as a subversive feminist tool, for, as a stage direction in another dramatic scene notes, "The writing is terrible plagiarism because all culture stinks and there's no reason to make new culture-stink" (137). The boss tells Janey, "You see, we own the language. Language must be used clearly and precisely to reveal our universe" (136). He verifies Janey's belief that she is trapped by masculine language and institutions. In this passage, it almost seems as though Acker is inserting herself as author, emphasizing her refusal to be bound by conventional language and forms of expression. Because Acker is known for reusing extant literature, she subversively comments on Janey's frustration with being bound by male forms of expression.

Both novels criticize Western philosophy, and other scholars have noticed this critique. Marjorie Worthington, for example, argues that Acker "highlights the constructed and artificial nature of the very binaries by which we make sense of the world" (392). Likewise, Daniel Punday notices that "Acker shares with [Elizabeth] Grosz the attempt to complicate the body/mind and self/other oppositions" (8). Accordingly, Abhor critiques the Western ideal of reason:

Logocentrism and idealism, theology, all supports of the repressive society. Property's pillars. Reason which always homogenizes and reduces, represses and unifies phenomena or actuality into what can be perceived and so controlled. The subjects, us, are now stable and socializable. Reason is always in the service of the political and economic masters. It is here that literature strikes, at this base, where

the concepts and actings of order impose themselves. Literature is that which
denounces and slashes apart the repressing machine at the level of the signified.
(12)

Acker seems to insert herself again as author, noting that literature allows her
to attack Western philosophy and Enlightenment ideals of reason,
objectivity, and the unified being.

Similarly, Abhor defines "being" as "mentality, feeling, physicality"
(133). She argues that the part of "being" that is "free of all control" is our
"unconscious" (133-34). Because the unconscious is "free of control," it is
"our only defence against institutionalized meaning, institutionalized
language, control, fixation, judgement, prison" (134). In other words, all
parts of human existence, with the exception of the unconscious, are subject
to social control. But Abhor argues that historical memory can contest some
social institutions, for "[t]o remember is to beat war" (112). Memory,
therefore, is a weapon of survival, without which we lose an element of
identity. For Abhor observes, "I no longer remembered. Without my
memory I realized reality was gone" (112-113). As these passages show,
memory is part of being; Abhor undermines Western philosophy and the
body-mind division that comes with it. She then criticizes, as Janey does, the
use of language as a dominating and oppressive force:

> Ten years ago it seemed possible to destroy language which normalizes and controls
> by cutting that language. Nonsense would attack the empire-making (empirical)
> empire of language, the prisons of meaning.
>
> But this nonsense, since it depended on sense, simply pointed back to the
> normalizing institutions.
>
> What is the language of the 'unconscious'? (If this ideal unconscious or freedom
> doesn't exist: pretend it does, use fiction, for the sake of survival, all of our
> survival.) Its primary language must be taboo, all that is forbidden. Thus, an attack
> on the institutions of prison via language would demand the use of a language or
> languages which aren't acceptable, which are forbidden. Language, on one level,
> constitutes a set of codes and social and historical agreements. Nonsense doesn't
> per se break down the codes; speaking precisely that which the codes forbid breaks
> the codes. (134)

This theoretical passage solidifies Abhor's and in fact Acker's view of
language as an institution. It recalls the Diseuse's trauma in speaking a
forced language in *Dictée* (3), and it echoes Janey's complaint in *Blood and
Guts* that women must speak with a masculine language (132). Yet in the

above passage, Abhor further observes that language can be used to subvert some systemic problems (such as "prison," which we have seen as recurring themes in both *Blood and Guts* and *Empire*) but that only "unacceptable" language can do so. Therefore, in order to "break the codes" of "normalizing institutions," women must breach taboos. Indeed, Acker's subversive use of graphic sex, incest, plagiarism, and violence does just that. By breaching taboos and writing about perverse and incendiary subjects, Acker effectively recaptures language as a feminist, resistant force.

Acker's works, particularly *Blood and Guts* and *Empire*, demonstrate that the lack of women's bonds leads to perpetual fragmentation. I include them in this study because they provide excellent contrasts to the other novels, which portray the healing that is often paired with the recognition of shared wounds. While the other novels in this study effectively demonstrate women's bonds as viable means of contesting patriarchy, Acker's novels show the alternative. They reveal how the lack of women's bonds will perpetuate oppressions of gender, race, and class. However, this is not to say that Acker's works are somehow less resistant or subversive. In fact, Acker's novels provide some of the most resistant, subversive, and empowering criticisms of intertwined forms of oppression, particularly sexism, racism, heteronormativity, and capitalism. Acker herself lived this resistance, and her work is a controversial, difficult, and discomfiting attack on intertwining oppressions, demonstrating, through their absence, how feminist bonds might contest these oppressions.

✻ CONCLUSION

Resistance and Feminist Healing

As Susan Bordo argues, "We desperately need an effective political discourse about the female body, a discourse adequate to an analysis of the insidious, and often paradoxical, pathways of modern social control" (167). Indeed, the female body involves and requires a new discourse, for it has been manipulated, constructed, controlled, and distorted by various social and political forces. In *Beloved, Dictée, Stigmata, Corregidora, Gulf Dreams, The Woman Who Owned the Shadows, Blood and Guts in High School,* and *Empire of the Senseless,* we see the female body continuously exposed to force and control by patriarchal, racist, classist, and heteronormative regimes. These bodies are enslaved, beaten, raped, and tortured, becoming literal testimonies to the various oppressions women face. The novels give voice to the silenced and oppressed, portraying narratively these experiences, and it is the textual representation of corporeal experience that sets these novels apart from many of their contemporaries. One of the most striking examples is Lizzie DuBose, who must discover what her great-great-grandmother underwent in order to understand her heritage fully. *Stigmata* reminds us that we always stand at some distance from these events, that we can never fully participate in the unique and complex realities of other women. We are reminded that only the most literal and physical of re-experiencing can allow us to understand completely the dehumanization and torture to which Ayo and other enslaved people were subjected.

But the novels also remind us that the feminist struggle must go on. Lizzie's twentieth-century reliving of a brutal moment in American slavery shows that the legacy continues—that while slavery was technically ended in the nineteenth century, innumerable familial heritages have been forever lost, and discrimination and racism persist. Because the struggle continues, these novels are largely resistant and empowering, and while they focus on the past, they call for a better future, encouraging the contemporary reader to engage in the struggle for full equality. Likewise, the female protagonists in these novels carry on the battle, allowing their bodies to feel the full force of history, and then struggling, if possible, to share these experiences with their mothers, grandmothers, female lovers, and female friends. In other words, while the female body in these novels has been tortured and maimed, it has also become the site, tool, and product of feminist resistance and empowerment. The historical wounds and scars that are etched on these bodies generally indicate that the women will go through or have gone through a process of healing. Moreover, the ultimate recognition of shared wounds, in most of the novels, shows the reclamation of matrilineal or women's connection that has so often been erased in history.

What I hope to have communicated in this study is not a general way of reading postmodern multiethnic American women's novels, but rather, a way of reading these particular novels, paired for their shared thematic concerns and then placed into a larger conversation with each other. Further, I hope to have generated an extension to the extant work on this literature by connecting disjointed, postmodern narrative to the theories surrounding the female body. My reading of this literature finds that the fragmented female body is both a site and a product of historical forces—a symbol of those oppressions that have forcefully marked female identity. Yet the body is also an active agent in (re)connecting women. The literature urges community, sisterhood, and matrilineage as potential solutions to this fragmentation, for only female connections in these novels allow for healing or at least the pretext for healing. As Laurie Vickroy has poignantly argued, the scars of fictional characters often provide "connecting points" between characters (32). While I have agreed with Vickroy throughout this study, I hope I have taken the discussion further by examining the additional layers of ethnicity, gender, class, and sexuality.

The trajectory of this study has moved us from the matriarchal families of *Beloved* and *Dictée* to the patriarchal families of *Blood and Guts* and *Empire*. Along the way, each of these novels has presented readers with ways of connecting with women to contest historical and contemporary oppressions. Toni Morrison's *Beloved* and Theresa Hak Kyung Cha's *Dictée* remind us of the complex but vital relationships we have with our own mothers. The recognition between daughters and their mothers, or other maternal figures such as Baby Suggs, provides the initial and ongoing means of healing. Importantly, the legacy of oppression remains with many women in their modern-day lives, as Phyllis Alesia Perry's *Stigmata* and Gayl Jones's *Corregidora* demonstrate. Yet, by understanding the historical narratives of their matrilineage, ambivalent and violent as those histories may be, these women come to an ultimate understanding of their own identities, which are inextricably intertwined with their oppressed but resistant foremothers. However, several of the characters examined in this study do not show the trajectory of feminist (re)connection found in *Beloved*, *Dictée*, *Stigmata*, and *Corregidora*. Rather, Emma Pérez's *Gulf Dreams* and Paula Gunn Allen's *The Woman Who Owned the Shadows* demonstrate the wounding caused by heteronormative failure to recognize bonds formed between women who are coerced into silence and invisibility. Likewise, Kathy Acker's *Blood and Guts* and *Empire* stand as a testament to the chaos, confusion, and loss of identity that emerge when women are entirely bereft of female connections, whether this absence is by choice or not. Yet the lack of connections is not meant to present an immobilizing force. Rather, the novels encourage women's bonds as a valuable way of contesting the kinds of patriarchal restrictions that these characters otherwise encounter. In every case, as complex and different as they may be, the bonds suggested in each of these novels are presented as necessary to feminism's ongoing struggle.

Again, the fragmented female body is not a positive force but is the symbol of a long history of oppression. It recalls Mary Wollstonecraft Shelley's tragic female creation, whose sheer existence is precluded when she is destroyed by the doctor. However, what postmodern multiethnic American women's novels add to this concept is the possibility for recognition and resistance. Although bonds with men can be powerful, fulfilling, and restorative relationships—as in the relationship between Lizzie DuBose and Anthony Paul, Sethe and Paul D, or perhaps Ursa and Mutt—we see the strongest connections forged between women. Indeed, these novels suggest that it is through the shared recognition and understanding of historical fragmentation that women can begin to heal one another.

I close by reflecting that each of the novels in this study presents the body as a remembering entity, as an element of self that is not only physical, but also psychological, spiritual, intellectual, emotional. Because the body is a conscious element in these novels, the novelists break down the conventional Western dichotomy between body and mind, a dichotomy which legitimizes the male-female hierarchy. Therefore, the larger suggestion here is that we should begin to view the body as a primary element of selfhood, as a remembering entity, and in fact, as a testament to our experiences. We must move beyond the Western philosophical denigration of the body, for the body is, undeniably, what defines us as humans, what brings us into existence, and what allows us to experience the world. To move forward, these writers ultimately suggest, we should continue to resist dominant ideologies and challenge the status quo, for these forces tend to perpetuate oppression based on gender, race, class, ethnicity, geography, and sexuality. The writers suggest that hope is available to us, that all women, like the young girl at the end of *Dictée*, can also be "lifted up," if only our female communities will work together.

❈ NOTES

1   Gregson echoes my belief that "Fredric Jameson's insistence on a 'new depthlessness' looks entirely misplaced in this context" of Morrison's historicizing (89). He also believes women's postmodern fiction is highly political: "Much of the feminist fiction writing in the postmodern period has been so explicitly political that it has mingled fictive modes with discursive ones and so has constituted one of the most important cultural forces in the period which have tellingly tested generic boundaries" (105).

2   Although recent style guidelines have eliminated the need for brackets around ellipses, I retain brackets in this book to clarify which ellipses exist in the quoted text and which do not. This choice was made because many of the primary works in this study use ellipses stylistically within the novel's text. Therefore, those ellipses that appear within square brackets are my own insertions, while those ellipses without brackets appear in the original quoted text.

3   For a discussion of the connections and conflicts between feminism and realism, see Rita Felski's *Beyond Feminist Aesthetics: Feminist Literature and Social Change*.

4   An examination of capitalism and the rivalries it enforces are beyond the scope of my study. See Silvia Federici's *Caliban and the Witch* for an examination of the interconnections between capitalism and patriarchy.

5   To be fair, another reading of Scarry is possible here. Scarry also argues, "To have pain is to have *certainty*; to hear about pain is to have *doubt*" (13). Therefore, she may be correct if we interpret the healers here as having experienced the same pain themselves. Baby Suggs, for example, can heal Sethe not because she hears about Sethe's pain, but because she herself has actually endured the same pain. This reading is also valid, though it negates the nuance of each woman's specific trauma.

6   Tan's novel is outside the scope of my study not only due to space constraints, but also because I believe *The Joy Luck Club* is not as subversive, postmodern, feminist, and resistant as the other novels examined here.

7   I am indebted to Grosz for the Western philosophical framework here: Plato, Aristotle, Descartes, Christianity.

8   Many critics deal with motherhood and maternal bonds in *Beloved*. These critics include Naomi Morgenstern, Erica Lawson, Lucille P. Fultz, and Barbara Offutt Mathieson. Of note here is Lorraine Liscio, who discusses Baby Suggs's "maternal 'absolute' powers of healing" (38), and Stephanie A. Demetrakopoulos, who notes the "dangers of mothering to the individuation of the mother herself" (52). Shu-li Chang and Ashraf H. A. Rushdy, importantly, examine the importance of daughters to history. Carol E. Henderson's *Scarring the Black Body* and Dennis Patrick Slattery's *The Wounded Body: Remembering the Markings of Flesh* also provide discussions of *Beloved*'s fragmented bodies.

9   For more on the Margaret Garner story, see Rushdy's "Daughters" and Fultz.

10   I am aware that I neglect men's wounds and scars, which are also significant, though they lie outside the range of my argument. *Beloved*'s Paul D bears many wounds and scars, though he fails to achieve empathy. Moreover, while Paul D initially drives out Beloved as a symbolic wound, she later drives him out, showing that he has not moved beyond his own wounds. In *Stigmata*, there is some suggestion that Anthony Paul is part of Lizzie's historical experiences, though his body is free from wounding. But unlike Paul D, Anthony Paul finds beauty in the scarring of Lizzie's back (147). In *Corregidora*, we learn that Mutt and Tadpole endure their own families' legacies of slavery, though their bodies seem free of the effects. In *Gulf Dreams*, the narrator "found reprieve with Juan" (65), a young man wounded in the Vietnam War: "Humbly, he expressed himself with a body scarred and a memory wounded from horrors in Vietnam" (65). The narrator is drawn to Juan's scarred body, showing her desire to recognize and connect with others: "As I kiss each rupture of flesh, wanting to heal that which I cannot touch, I fall in love with his map" (67). Yet Juan's wounds are not shared with the narrator—they arise from different sources and require different forms of healing. Also, Inocencio is fraught with a history of abuse, incest, and repressed homosexuality. At the end of the novel, Inocencio is violently beaten to death outside a bar, another fragmented victim of the heteronormative expectations of the community: "The loud rapist had been beaten to death [....] Flattened, pale testicles with dried cakes of blood were jammed into Inocencio's mouth" (154). Although Inocencio's death should provide some form of poetic justice, it is, in fact, quite tragic. While his actions are in no way defensible, he is ultimately a product, a perpetuator, and a victim of the same heteronormative forces that fragment the sexualities of the women of *Gulf Dreams*. In Acker's works, on the contrary, men's bodies are rarely fragmented, and when they are, it is only to represent Abhor's belief that the body is the mirror of the mind (65), and hence, oppressive patriarchal

practices make many men hideous in Acker's works. For example, in *Blood and Guts*, President Carter is given a vivid and grotesque bodily description. In *Empire*, Thivai imagines his own fragmentation by his mother in a vision (106), but this vision seems irrelevant, because Thivai actually kills his mother: "I murdered you: I cut through the red blood that united your mouth and mine [....] So now there's no more you. So now there's no more mommy. Men killed you off. Since I'm a man, I killed you off. I killed you" (106). The idea seems to be that men are incapable of being fragmented by women. Hence, while men, too, often have wounds representative of historical oppressions, they are generally not drawn into a circle or web of understanding and healing.

11 Other critics have made the point that the community of women is what helps drive Beloved out. Rushdy, for example, notes the "healing and wholeness" provided by "their communal lives" ("Daughters" 574). He also notes that Ella "offers Sethe the opportunity to reclaim herself. In the end Sethe does, and does so by an act of community" ("Daughters" 584). Similarly, Morgenstern argues that "*Beloved* stresses the importance of extra-familial community" (117).

12 Quite a bit of scholarship exists on Cha's *Dictée*. However, most of the work published on *Dictée* tends to focus on the construction of Korean American identity and narrative form. The most thorough examinations of *Dictée* are provided by Elaine H. Kim and Norma Alarcón's edited collection and Lisa Lowe's study of *Dictée* in *Immigrant Acts*. Scott Swaner discusses the colonial narrative's connection to the body, and Elisabeth A. Frost connects Cha's visual narrative to the politics of the body. Florence Hsiao-ching Li's reading stands alone in examining the connections of motherhood and the motherland in *Dictée*. Thus, the extant scholarship on Cha's strongly feminist and highly significant novel has not adequately addressed the specific issue of bodily fragmentation and matrilineal bonds. Also particularly helpful is Kun Jong Lee's explanation of *Dictée* as a subversive rewriting of Hesiod's *Catalogue of Women*. Similarly, Stella Oh and Juliana Spahr deal with the writing style as an empowering and liberating practice of (re)claiming identity. In addition, Beth Berila makes the important argument that "experimental" literature is experimental only to the degree that it contrasts with conventional, Western writing. Other critics deal with Cha's writing style as a specifically diasporic narrative choice. For example, Srimati Mukherjee connects immigration to the text produced by a diasporic identity, while Josephine Nock-Hee Park describes cultural boundaries in America. Meanwhile, critics including Sue J. Kim and Thy Phu deal with the politics of Cha's style, focusing on the visual text and the literary apparatus Cha uses.

13 Significantly, the punctuation also disappears between the labels given to Yu Guan Soon: "Child revolutionary child patriot woman soldier deliverer of nation" (37). As Braidotti's idea of "nomadic consciousness" points out, shifting identities might be a viable means for political resistance (22, 25). The disappearance of punctuation indicates the multiple roles or shifting identities that Guan Soon plays, and thus she has a "critical consciousness that resists settling into socially coded modes of thought and behavior" (Braidotti 5).

14 Another observation about the significance of motherhood can be seen in the book's frontispiece, which shows Korean inscriptions on a wall. The *han'g* script translates "mother" (*i*), "I want to see you" (*pogosip'da*), "I'm hungry" (*paega kop'ayo*), and "I want to go home" (*kagosipta, kohyang-e*), according to Swaner (59). These inscriptions point out the central role not only of the mother, but also of the body, or, according to Swaner's helpful insight, "the absence of the body, or the absence of the free subject's body, or at least the absence of the subject's body from its mother" (59). The inscriptions present "the themes of mother/child, longing, hunger, nostalgia, and absence before the book even begins" (Swaner 59). Discussing the same inscriptions, Frost notes, "Rendered in the language outlawed by Korea's colonizer, the message is inescapably clear, at least to those who can recognize the signs: loss of one's native land evinces a pain as sharp, as physical, as bodily hunger" (181). Had Frost included the simple phrase "motherland" instead of "native land," she could have captured Cha's message, "your mother your home," and the idea that one's mother *is* one's home (49).

15 The term "neo-slave narrative" is coined by Bernard W. Bell in *The Afro-American Novel and Its Tradition*. It is used to describe a "modern" story of "escape from bondage to freedom" (289).

16 In one study, Lisa A. Long appropriately connects *Stigmata* to Octavia Butler's novel *Kindred*, and in another study, Stefanie Sievers argues for the importance of maintaining family history, painful as it may be.

17 Much of the scholarship focuses on the novel's structure and use of time, specifically the meaning and repetition of history; included in this category are articles by Elizabeth Swanson Goldberg, Casey Clabough, and Bruce Simon. Ashraf H. A. Rushdy discusses desire and resistance in the novel, while Thomas Fahy explores sexuality and Ursa's homophobia, arguing that she cannot escape the patriarchal logic of her foremothers (213). Studies by Patricia Muñoz Cabrera and Jennifer Griffiths focus on the female body in the novel. Elizabeth Yukins, Naomi Morgenstern, Madhu Dubey, Caroline Streeter, Cheryl Wall, and Gil Zehava Hochberg focus on motherhood and matrilineage.

18 See Amanda J. Davis and Janice Harris for a fuller discussion of the patriarchal repetition of reproduction that the Corregidora women face.

19 The perspective provided by trauma theory is also relevant here. Cathy Caruth describes "literal repetition" as "an overwhelming occurrence [that] remains in its insistent return, absolutely true to the event" (4). According to Naomi Morgenstern, "What is at stake in Caruth's analysis, then, is not so much the *possibility* of history as its *preservation*. If trauma endangers the subject, it would seem to keep 'history' safe" (104). Indeed, Lizzie's experiences endanger her well-being, as she is found bleeding nearly to death on her bedroom floor after keenly and personally experiencing Ayo's tragic whipping. What is more interesting in Morgenstern's analysis, however, is the idea that "a repetition addressed to and heard by another becomes testimonial" (105). In other words, if these experiences can be shared, the understanding of collective cultural wounds is created. By helping her mother understand, Lizzie feels she can both connect to her mother and keep history "safe."

20 Other critics have noted Ursa's use of song to continue her story. Wall points out that Ursa determines to make "her art the legacy that she will leave instead of the children her ancestors commanded her to bear" (120). Similarly, Boutry argues that Ursa "turns to music and song as her own proof and testimony. Hers will not be a straightforward reproduction, but rather an original *composition*" (110).

21 The exception is Son Jackson, who shows his understanding when he asks Eva, "Is she [Lizzie] one of you?" (218). Anthony Paul eventually accepts, and even participates on some level, in Lizzie's story. Yet he never fully understands it, saying near the end of the novel, "I gotta deal with this reincarnation junk" (223). Clearly he accepts and wants to believe, but in his frustration, he says that Lizzie "just might" lose him (224). Moreover, Lizzie's decision to move to Atlanta despite Anthony Paul's protest indicates that the (re)connection with male characters is not of primary significance. It also suggests that Lizzie might choose not to reproduce her lineage.

22 As Dubey argues, "[I]nternalizing the slave master's creed, the Corregidora women discourage their female descendants from engaging in any heterosexual relation that does not fulfill reproductive ends" (256). Morgenstern notes that the novel "confronts the fact that cultural transmission entails the burden of being compelled to repeat the past with one's own life" (107). As Boutry notes, "[T]he women's reaction to this memory [of Simon Corregidora] is to inculcate Ursa with their history and to urge her to have daughters to perpetuate this oral tradition" (106). In a slightly different vein, Harris argues, "Ursa is taught to make love in order to keep alive an historical tale of rape" (2).

23 A few articles, including those by Ellie Hernández and Lourdes Torres, focus on desire and violence in the novel. Hernández foregrounds ethnicity in her article, which notes, "The novel itself seems to embody a different historical account of the cultural representation of Chicana lesbian sexuality by making visible the traumatic psychological ruptures of colonial memory in Chicana/o discourse" (155). Hernández also helpfully connects the novel's disjointed style to ethnicity, gender, and sexuality, noting that "Pérez creates an aesthetic of fragmentation that is directed at the failure of cultural nationalism to recuperate from the colonial violence an actualization of Chicana female autonomy as sexual subjects" (158). In a different vein, Torres addresses the interconnections of oppressions in the novel, arguing that "remembering" in *Gulf Dreams* provides "recognition of the connections among individual and collective oppression" (228).

24 The scant scholarship on *The Woman Who Owned the Shadows*, including articles by Tara Prince-Hughes, Barbara Cook, and Vanessa Holford, focuses mainly on Ephanie's quest for identity and memory.

25 It is important to note that contemporary women's literature does not simply relegate lesbian women to the tragic position we see in *Gulf Dreams*. Writers such as Alice Walker, Rita Mae Brown, Jeanette Winterson, and others portray lesbian relationships that successfully come to fruition. The novels I have selected for this study were chosen because they demonstrate the need for women's bonds, without which these protagonists feel incomplete.

26 Interestingly, we never see Elena in the present moment; we know her only as she is shaped through Ephanie's memory and dreams.

27 Christina Milletti, Karen Brennan, Kathleen Hulley, Larry McCaffery, and John N. Duvall explore Acker's difficult narrative style. Christopher Kocela, Nicole Cooley, Marjorie Worthington, Kevin Floyd, Arthur F. Redding, and David Brande discuss the body. Only Jon Stratton suggests Acker's Jewish heritage as it influences her fiction. Few critics, Susan E. Hawkins and Kathy Hughes among them, have focused on the role of families and fathers. But when it comes to discussing Acker's fictional mothers and female characters, or lack thereof, scholars have been largely silent. Even Colleen Kennedy's article "Simulating Sex and Imagining Mothers" does not complicate female relationships, but rather, examines whether "simulations of pornographic sexual relations free women from object-status in the culture," concluding that Acker fails to move the reader beyond "violence" (183-84). Peter Wollen notes that in Acker's books, the mother figure is a "tragic ruin" (8), though he does not explore mothers any further.

28 See Brennan for an examination of "The World" section of *Blood and Guts*.

29 Some critics read *Empire* as a re-appropriation of *Huckleberry Finn*. See, for example, Carla Harryman's "Acker Un-Formed," in which she notes that Abhor is akin to Huck Finn himself (41); and of course, *Blood and Guts* appropriates *The Scarlet Letter*, among other texts.

❋ BIBLIOGRAPHY

Works by Primary Authors

Acker, Kathy. "Apparatus and Memory: A Conversation with Kathy Acker." Interview with Benjamin Bratton. *Speed: Technology, Media, Society* 1.1 (1994): 26 pars. Web. 8 Feb. 2009.

———. *Blood and Guts in High School*. 1978. New York: Grove Weidenfeld, 1989. Print.

———. *Bodies of Work: Essays by Kathy Acker*. London: Serpent's Tail, 1997. Print.

———. *Empire of the Senseless*. New York: Grove, 1988. Print.

———. "A Few Notes on Two of My Books." *The Review of Contemporary Fiction* 9.3 (1989): 31-36. Print.

Allen, Paula Gunn. Introduction. *Song of the Turtle: American Indian Literature, 1974-1994*. Ed. Paula Gunn Allen. New York: Ballantine, 1996. 3-17. Print.

———. *Off the Reservation: Reflections on Boundary-Busting, Border-Crossing Loose Canons*. Boston: Beacon, 1998. Print.

———. *The Woman Who Owned the Shadows*. 1985. San Francisco: Aunt Lute, 1994. Print.

Cha, Theresa Hak Kyung. *Dictée*. 1982. Berkeley: University of California Press, 2001. Print.

Jones, Gayl. *Corregidora*. Boston: Beacon, 1975. Print.

———. "Gayl Jones Takes a Look at *Corregidora*—An Interview." Interview with Roseann P. Bell. *Sturdy Black Bridges: Visions of Black Women in Literature*. Eds. Roseann P. Bell, Bettye J. Parker, and Beverly Guy-Sheftall. Garden City: Anchor/Doubleday, 1979. 282-87. Print.

Morrison, Toni. *Beloved*. 1987. New York: Plume, 1998. Print.

———. "Unspeakable Things Unspoken: The Afro-American Presence in American Literature." *Michigan Quarterly Review* 28.1 (1989): 1-34. Print.

Pérez, Emma. *Gulf Dreams*. Berkeley: Third Woman, 1996. Print.

Perry, Phyllis Alesia. *Stigmata*. New York: Anchor, 1999. Print.

Works by Others

Anzaldúa, Gloria. *Borderlands, La Frontera: The New Mestiza*. San Francisco: Spinsters/Aunt Lute, 1987. Print.

———. *Making Face, Making Soul, Haciendo Caras: Creative and Critical Perspectives by Feminists of Color*. San Francisco: Aunt Lute, 1990. Print.

Aristotle. "Generation of Animals." *The Complete Works of Aristotle*. Revised Oxford Translation. Vol. 1. Ed. Jonathan Barnes. Princeton: Princeton UP, 1985. Print.

Baldwin, James. "The White Man's Guilt." *James Baldwin: Collected Essays*. Ed. Toni Morrison. Library of America, 1998. 722-27. Print.

Bell, Bernard W. *The Afro-American Novel and Its Tradition*. Amherst: University of Massachusetts Press, 1987. Print.

Bell-Scott, Patricia, ed. *Double Stitch: Black Women Write about Mothers and Daughters*. Boston: Beacon, 1991. Print.

Berila, Beth. "Unsettling Calls for National Unity: The Pedagogy of Experimental Multiethnic Literatures." *MELUS: The Journal of the Society for the Study of the Multi-Ethnic Literature of the United States* 30.2 (2005): 31-47. Print.

Bomberger, Ann. "The Efficacy of Shock for Feminist Politics: Kathy Acker's *Blood and Guts in High School* and Donald Barthelme's *Snow White*." *Gender Reconstructions: Pornography and Perversions in Literature and Culture*. Eds. Cindy L. Carlson, Robert L. Mazzola, and Susan M. Bernardo. Aldershot, England: Ashgate, 2002. 189-204. Print.

Bordo, Susan. *Unbearable Weight: Feminism, Western Culture, and the Body*. Berkeley: University of California Press, 1995. Print.

Boutry, Katherine. "Black and Blue: The Female Body of Blues Writing in Jean Toomer, Toni Morrison, and Gayl Jones." *Black Orpheus: Music in African American Fiction from the Harlem Renaissance to Toni Morrison*. New York: Garland, 2000. 91-118. Print.

Braidotti, Rosi. *Nomadic Subjects: Embodiment in Contemporary Feminist Theory*. New York: Columbia UP, 1994. Print.

Brande, David. "Making Yourself a Body without Organs: The Cartography of Pain in Kathy Acker's *Don Quixote*." *Genre: Forms of Discourse and Culture* 24.2 (1991): 191-209. Print.

Brennan, Karen. "The Geography of Enunciation: Hysterical Pastiche in Kathy Acker's Fiction." *Boundary 2: An International Journal of Literature and Culture* 21.2 (1994): 243-68. Print.

Burrows, Victoria. *Whiteness and Trauma: The Mother-Daughter Knot in the Fiction of Jean Rhys, Jamaica Kincaid, and Toni Morrison.* New York: Palgrave Macmillan, 2004. Print.

Butler, Judith. *Gender Trouble: Feminism and the Subversion of Identity.* New York: Routledge, 1990. Print.

———. *Undoing Gender.* New York: Routledge, 2004. Print.

Butler, Octavia. *Kindred.* Boston: Beacon, 2003. Print.

Caruth, Cathy. Introduction. *American Imago* 48 (1991): 1-12. Print.

Chang, Shu-li. "Daughterly Haunting and Historical Traumas: Toni Morrison's *Beloved* and Jamaica Kincaid's *The Autobiography of My Mother.*" *Concentric: Literary and Cultural Studies* 30.2 (2004): 105-27. Print.

Cixous, Hélène. "The Laugh of the Medusa." Trans. Keith Cohen and Paula Cohen. *Signs: Journal of Women in Culture and Society* 1.4 (1976): 875-93. Print.

Clabough, Casey. "'Toward an All-Inclusive Structure': The Early Fiction of Gayl Jones." *Callaloo: A Journal of African Diaspora Arts and Letters* 29.2 (2006): 634-57. Print.

Collins, Patricia Hill. "The Meaning of Motherhood in Black Culture and Black Mother-Daughter Relationships." Bell-Scott 42-60. Print.

———. "Shifting the Center: Race, Class, and Feminist Theorizing about Motherhood." *Representations of Motherhood.* Eds. Donna Bassin, Margaret Honey, and Meryle Mahrer Kaplan. New Haven: Yale UP, 1994. 56-74. Print.

Cook, Barbara. "Ephanie's Vision Quest: Blending Native American and Feminist Elements." *Reclaiming Native American Cultures.* Eds. Annette Trefzer and Robin L. Murray. Durant: Southeastern Oklahoma State University, 1998. 20-27. Print.

Cooley, Nicole. "Painful Bodies: Kathy Acker's Last Texts." Hinton and Hogue 193-202. Print.

Cosslett, Tess. "Feminism, Matrilinealism, and the 'House of Women' in Contemporary Women's Fiction." *Journal of Gender Studies* 5.1 (1996): 7-17. Print.

Daly, Mary. *Pure Lust: Elemental Feminist Philosophy.* Boston: Beacon, 1984. Print.

Davis, Amanda J. "To Build a Nation: Black Women Writers, Black Nationalism, and the Violent Reduction of Wholeness." *Frontiers: A Journal of Women Studies* 26.3 (2005): 24-53. Print.

Davis, Angela Y. *Women, Race, and Class.* New York: Random House, 1981. Print.

Deleuze, Gilles, and Félix Guattari. *A Thousand Plateaus: Capitalism and Schizophrenia*. Trans. Brian Massumi. Minneapolis: University of Minnesota Press, 1987. Print.

Demetrakopoulos, Stephanie A. "Maternal Bonds as Devourers of Women's Individuation in Toni Morrison's *Beloved*." *African American Review* 26.1 (1992): 51-59. Print.

Derrida, Jacques. *Dissemination*. Trans. Barbara Johnson. Chicago: Chicago UP, 1981. Print.

Descartes, René. *The Philosophical Writings of Descartes*. Vol. II. Trans. John Cottinghand, Robert Stoothoff, and Dugald Murdoch. Cambridge: Cambridge UP, 1984. Print.

Di Prete, Laura. *"Foreign Bodies": Trauma, Corporeality, and Textuality in Contemporary American Literature and Culture*. New York: Routledge, 2006. Print.

Dick, Leslie. "Seventeen Paragraphs on Kathy Acker." Scholder, Harryman, and Ronell 110-16. Print.

D'Lugo, Carol Clark. *The Fragmented Novel in Mexico: The Politics of Form*. Austin: University of Texas Press, 1997. Print.

Dubey, Madhu. "Gayl Jones and the Matrilineal Metaphor of Tradition." *Signs: Journal of Women in Culture and Society* 20.2 (1995): 245-67. Print.

Duvall, John N. "Parody or Pastiche? Kathy Acker, Toni Morrison, and the Critical Appropriation of Faulknerian Masculinity." *The Faulkner Journal* 15.1-2 (1999-2000): 169-84. Print.

Everingham, Christine. *Motherhood and Modernity: An Investigation into the Rational Dimension of Mothering*. Buckingham, PA: Open UP, 1994. Print.

Fahy, Thomas. "Unsilencing Lesbianism in the Early Fiction of Gayl Jones." Mills and Mitchell 203-20. Print.

Federici, Silvia. *Caliban and the Witch*. New York: Autonomedia, 2004. Print.

Felski, Rita. *Beyond Feminist Aesthetics: Feminist Literature and Social Change*. Cambridge: Harvard UP, 1989. Print.

Floyd, Kevin. "Deconstructing Masochism in Kathy Acker's *Blood and Guts in High School* and Joyce Carol Oates's *You Must Remember This*." *Critical Studies on the Feminist Subject*. Ed. Giovanna Covi. Trento, Italy: Dipartimento di Scienze Filologiche e Storiche, Università degli Studi di Trento, 1997. 57-77. Print.

Franco, Dean. *Ethnic American Literature: Comparing Chicano, Jewish, and African American Writing*. Charlottesville: University of Virginia Press, 2006. Print.

Fraser, Nancy, and Linda J. Nicholson. "Social Criticism without Philosophy: An Encounter between Feminism and Postmodernism." Nicholson 19-38. Print.

Frost, Elisabeth A. "'In Another Tongue': Body, Image, Text in Theresa Hak Kyung Cha's *Dictée*." Hinton and Hogue 181-92. Print.

Fultz, Lucille P. "Images of Motherhood in Toni Morrison's *Beloved*." Bell-Scott 32-41. Print.

García, Cristina. *Dreaming in Cuban*. New York: Ballantine, 1992. Print.

Gates, Jr., Henry Louis. *The Signifying Monkey: A Theory of Afro-American Literary Criticism*. New York: Oxford UP, 1988. Print.

Goldberg, Elizabeth Swanson. "Living the Legacy: Pain, Desire, and Narrative Time in Gayl Jones's *Corregidora*." *Callaloo: A Journal of African-American and African Arts and Letters* 26.2 (2003): 446-72. Print.

Gregson, Ian. *Postmodern Literature*. New York: Oxford UP, 2004. Print.

Griffiths, Jennifer. "Uncanny Spaces: Trauma, Cultural Memory, and the Female Body in Gayl Jones's *Corregidora* and Maxine Hong Kingston's *The Woman Warrior*." *Studies in the Novel* 38.3 (2006): 353-70. Print.

Grosz, Elizabeth. *Volatile Bodies: Toward a Corporeal Feminism*. Bloomington: Indiana UP, 1994. Print.

Haraway, Donna. "A Manifesto for Cyborgs: Science, Technology, and Socialist Feminism in the 1980s." Nicholson 190-233. Print.

Harris, Janice. "Gayl Jones's *Corregidora*." *Frontiers: A Journal of Women Studies* 5.3 (1981): 1-5. Print.

Harris, Trudier. Foreword. Mills and Mitchell ix-xiv. Print.

Harryman, Carla. "Acker Un-Formed." Scholder, Harryman, and Ronell 35-44. Print.

Hawkins, Susan E. "All in the Family: Kathy Acker's *Blood and Guts in High School*." *Contemporary Literature* 45.4 (2004): 637-58. Print.

Henderson, Carol E. *Scarring the Black Body: Race and Representation in African American Literature*. Columbia: University of Missouri Press, 2002. Print.

Hernández, Ellie. "Chronotope of Desire: Emma Pérez's *Gulf Dreams*." *Chicana Feminisms: A Critical Reader*. Eds. Gabriela F. Arredondo, Aida Hurtado, Norma Klahn, Olga Nájera-Ramírez, and Patricia Zavella. Durham: Duke UP, 2003. 155-77. Print.

Hinton, Laura, and Cynthia Hogue, eds. *We Who Love to Be Astonished: Experimental Women's Writing and Performance Poetics*. Tuscaloosa: University of Alabama Press, 2002. Print.

Hochberg, Gil Zehava. "Mother, Memory, History: Maternal Genealogies in Gayl Jones's *Corregidora* and Simone Schwarz-Bart's *Pluie et vent sur Télumée Miracle*." *Research in African Literatures* 34.2 (2003): 1-12. Print.

Holford, Vanessa. "Re Membering Ephanie: A Women's Re-Creation of Self in Paula Gunn Allen's *The Woman Who Owned the Shadows*." *Studies in American Indian Literatures: The Journal of the Association for the Study of American Indian Literatures* 6.1 (1994): 99-113. Print.

hooks, bell. *Communion: The Female Search for Love.* New York: Perennial, 2003. Print.

———. *Feminist Theory: From Margin to Center.* Boston: South End, 1984. Print.

Hsiao-ching Li, Florence. "Imagining the Mother/Motherland: Karen Tei Yamashita's *Tropic of Orange* and Theresa Hak Kyung Cha's *Dictée*." *Concentric: Literary and Cultural Studies* 30.1 (2004): 149-67. Print.

Hughes, Kathy. "Incest and Innocence: Janey's Youth in Kathy Acker's *Blood and Guts in High School*." *Nebula* 3.1 (2006): 122-31. Print.

Hulley, Kathleen. "Transgressing Genre: Kathy Acker's Intertext." *Intertextuality and Contemporary American Fiction.* Eds. Patrick O'Donnell and Robert Con Davis. Baltimore: Johns Hopkins UP, 1989. 171-90. Print.

Hurston, Zora Neale. *Their Eyes Were Watching God.* New York: Perennial, 1998. Print.

Jameson, Fredric. "Postmodernism and Consumer Society." *The Anti-Aesthetic: Essays on Postmodern Culture.* Ed. Hal Foster. Seattle: Bay, 1983. 111-25. Print.

———. *Postmodernism, Or, The Cultural Logic of Late Capitalism.* Durham: Duke UP, 1991. Print.

Kennedy, Colleen. "Simulating Sex and Imagining Mothers." *American Literary History* 4.1 (1992): 165-85. Print.

Kim, Elaine H., and Norma Alarcón, eds. *Writing Self, Writing Nation: A Collection of Essays on* Dictée *by Theresa Hak Kyung Cha.* Berkeley: Third Woman, 1994. Print.

Kim, Sue J. "*Apparatus*: Theresa Hak Kyung Cha and the Politics of Form." *Journal of Asian American Studies* 8.2 (2005): 143-69. Print.

Kocela, Christopher. "Resighting Gender Theory: Butler's Lesbian Phallus in Acker's *Pussy*." *LIT: Literature Interpretation Theory* 17.1 (2006): 77-104. Print.

Lawson, Erica. "Black Women's Mothering in a Historical and Contemporary Perspective: Understanding the Past, Forging the Future." *Mother Outlaws: Theories and Practices of Empowered Mothering.* Ed. Andrea O'Reilly. Toronto: Women's, 2004. 193-201. Print.

Lee, Kun Jong. "Rewriting Hesiod, Revisioning Korea: Theresa Hak Kyung Cha's *Dictée* as a Subversive Hesiodic Catalogue of Women." *College Literature* 33.3 (2006): 77-99. Print.

Liscio, Lorraine. "Beloved's Narrative: Writing Mother's Milk." *Tulsa Studies in Women's Literature.* 11.1 (1992): 31-46. Print.

Long, Lisa A. "A Relative Pain: The Rape of History in Octavia Butler's *Kindred* and Phyllis Alesia Perry's *Stigmata*." *College English* 64.4 (2002): 459-83. Print.

Lowe, Lisa. "Unfaithful to the Original: The Subject of *Dictée*." *Immigrant Acts: On Asian American Cultural Politics.* Durham, Duke UP, 1996. 128-53. Print.

Lyotard, Jean-Francois. *The Postmodern Condition: A Report on Knowledge.* Trans. Geoff Bennington and Brian Massumi. Theory and History of Literature Vol. 10. Minneapolis: University of Minnesota Press, 1984. Print.

Mathieson, Barbara Offutt. "Memory and Mother Love in Toni Morrison's *Beloved*." *American Imago: Studies in Psychoanalysis and Culture* 47.1 (1990): 1-21. Print.

McCaffery, Larry. "The Artists of Hell: Kathy Acker and 'Punk' Aesthetics." *Breaking the Sequence: Women's Experimental Fiction.* Ed. Ellen G. Friedman and Miriam Fuchs. Princeton: Princeton UP, 1989. 215-30. Print.

Merleau-Ponty, Maurice. *The Essential Writings of Merleau-Ponty.* Ed. Alden L. Fisher. New York: Harcourt, Brace, and World, 1969. Print.

Milletti, Christina. "Violent Acts, Volatile Words: Kathy Acker's Terrorist Aesthetic." *Studies in the Novel* 36.3 (2004): 352-73. Print.

Mills, Fiona, and Keith Mitchell, eds. *After the Pain: Critical Essays on Gayl Jones.* New York: Peter Lang, 2006. Print.

———. "After the Pain: An Introduction." Mills and Mitchell 1-10. Print.

Minh-ha, Trinh. *Woman, Native, Other: Writing Postcoloniality and Feminism.* Bloomington: Indiana UP, 1989. Print.

Morgenstern, Naomi. "Mother's Milk and Sister's Blood: Trauma and the Neo-Slave Narrative." *Differences: A Journal of Feminist Cultural Studies* 8.2 (1996): 101-26. Print.

Mukherjee, Srimati. "Nation, Immigrant, Text: Theresa Hak Kyung Cha's *Dictée*." *Transnational Asian American Literature: Sites and Transits.* Ed. Shirley Geok-lin Lim, et. al. Philadelphia: Temple UP, 2006. 197-215. Print.

Mulvey, Laura. *Visual and Other Pleasures.* New York: Palgrave, 1989. Print.

Muñoz Cabrera, Patricia. "(Em)Bodying the Flesh: Mythmaking and the Female Body in Gayl Jones' *Song for Anninho* and *Corregidora*." *PALARA: Publication of the Afro-Latin/American Research Association* 1 (1997): 106-16. Print.

Nicholson, Linda, ed. *Feminism/Postmodernism*. New York: Routledge, 1990. Print.

Oh, Stella. "The Enunciation of the Tenth Muse in Theresa Hak Kyung Cha's *Dictée*." *Lit: Literature Interpretation Theory* 13 (2002): 1-20. Print.

Park, Josephine Nock-Hee. "'What of the Partition': *Dictée*'s Boundaries and the American Epic." *Contemporary Literature* 46.2 (2005): 213-42. Print.

Phillips, Rod. "Purloined Letters: *The Scarlet Letter* in Kathy Acker's *Blood and Guts in High School*." *Critique: Studies in Contemporary Fiction* 35.3 (1994): 173-80. Print.

Phu, Thy. "Decapitated Forms: Theresa Hak Kyung Cha's Visual Text and the Politics of Visibility." *Mosaic: A Journal for the Interdisciplinary Study of Literature* 38.1 (2005): 17-36. Print.

Plato. *The Republic*. Trans. Allan Bloom. 2nd ed. Ithaca: Basic Books, 1991. Print.

Prince-Hughes, Tara. "Contemporary Two-Spirit Identity in the Fiction of Paula Gunn Allen and Beth Brant." *Studies in American Indian Literatures: The Journal of the Association for the Study of American Indian Literatures* 10.4 (1998): 9-31. Print.

Pryse, Marjorie. "Zora Neale Hurston, Alice Walker, and the 'Ancient Power' of Black Women." Introduction. *Conjuring: Black Women, Fiction, and Literary Tradition*. Eds. Marjorie Pryse and Hortense J. Spillers. Bloomington: Indiana UP, 1985. 1-24. Print.

Punday, Daniel. "Theories of Materiality and Location: Moving through Kathy Acker's *Empire of the Senseless*." *Genders* 27 (1998): 1-27. Print.

Redding, Arthur F. "Bruises, Roses: Masochism and the Writing of Kathy Acker." *Contemporary Literature* 35.2 (1994): 281-304. Print.

Rich, Adrienne. *Of Woman Born: Motherhood as Experience and Institution*. Tenth Anniversary Edition. New York: W. W. Norton, 1986. Print.

Rottenberg, Catherine. "*Passing*: Race, Identification, and Desire." *Criticism: A Quarterly for Literature and the Arts* 45.4 (2003): 435-52. Print.

Rushdy, Ashraf H. A. "Daughters Signifyin(g) History: The Example of Toni Morrison's *Beloved*." *American Literature: A Journal of Literary History, Criticism, and Bibliography* 64.3 (1992): 567-97. Print.

———. "'Relate Sexual to Historical': Race, Resistance, and Desire in Gayl Jones's *Corregidora*." *African American Review* 34.2: 273-97. Print.

Scarry, Elaine. *The Body in Pain: The Making and Unmaking of the World*. New York: Oxford UP, 1985. Print.

Scholder, Amy, Carla Harryman, and Avital Ronell, eds. *Lust for Life: On the Writings of Kathy Acker*. New York: Verso, 2006. Print.

Shelley, Mary Wollstonecraft. *Frankenstein, Or, The Modern Prometheus.* 1831. Hertfordshire: Wordsworth, 1999. Print.

Sievers, Stefanie. "Embodied Memories—Sharable Stories? The Legacies of Slavery as a Problem of Representation in Phyllis Alesia Perry's *Stigmata.*" *Monuments of the Black Atlantic: Slavery and Memory.* Eds. Joanne M. Braxton and Maria I. Diedrich. Piscataway, NJ, Transaction. 131-39. Print.

Simon, Bruce. "Traumatic Repetition: Gayl Jones's *Corregidora.*" *Race Consciousness: African-American Studies for the New Century.* Eds. Judith Jackson Fossett and Jeffrey A. Tucker. New York: New York UP, 1997. 93-112. Print.

Slattery, Dennis Patrick. *The Wounded Body: Remembering the Markings of Flesh.* Albany: State University of New York Press, 2000. Print.

Smith, Barbara. "Toward a Black Feminist Criticism." *The Truth That Never Hurts: Writings on Race, Gender, and Freedom.* New Brunswick: Rutgers UP, 2000. 3-21. Print.

Spahr, Juliana M. "Postmodernism, Readers, and Hak Kyung Cha's *Dictée.*" *College Literature* 23.3 (1996): 23-43. Print.

Stratton, Jon. "The Banality of Representation: Generation, Holocaust, Signification and *Empire of the Senseless.*" *New Formations: A Journal of Culture/Theory/Politics* 51 (2003-2004): 80-98. Print.

Streeter, Caroline. "Was Your Mama a Mulatto? Notes toward a Theory of Racialized Sexuality in Gayl Jones's *Corregidora* and Julie Dash's *Daughters of the Dust.*" *Callaloo: A Journal of African Diaspora Arts and Letters* 27.3 (2004): 768-87. Print.

Swaner, Scott. "Frustrating Colonial Narratives: Writing and the Body in *Dict.*" FJN Spec. Issue Two of *Atlantis: A Women's Studies Journal* (2004): 54-63. Orig. pub. *Asian Journal of Women's Studies* 3.2 (1997).

Tan, Amy. *The Joy Luck Club.* 1989. New York: Ivy, 1995. Print.

Torres, Lourdes. "Violence, Desire, and Transformative Remembering in Emma Pérez's *Gulf Dreams.*" *Tortilleras: Hispanic and U.S. Latina Lesbian Expression.* Eds. Lourdes Torres and Inmaculada Pertusa. Philadelphia: Temple UP, 2003. 228-39. Print.

Vickroy, Laurie. *Trauma and Survival in Contemporary Fiction.* Charlottesville: University of Virginia Press, 2002. Print.

Walker, Alice. *In Search of Our Mother's Gardens: Womanist Prose.* San Diego: Harcourt Brace Jovanovich, 1983. Print.

Wall, Cheryl A. *Worrying the Line: Black Women Writers, Lineage, and Literary Tradition.* Chapel Hill: University of North Carolina Press, 2005. Print.

Watten, Barrett. "Foucault Reads Acker and Rewrites the History of the Novel." Scholder, Harryman, and Ronell 58-77. Print.

Wollen, Peter. "Kathy Acker." Scholder, Harryman, and Ronell 1-11. Print.

Worthington, Marjorie. "'The Territory Named Women's Bodies': The Public and Pirate Spaces of Kathy Acker." *LIT: Literature Interpretation Theory* 15 (2004): 389-408. Print.

Yu, Yi-Lin. *Mother, She Wrote: Matrilineal Narratives in Contemporary Women's Writing*. New York: Peter Lang, 2005. Print.

Yukins, Elizabeth. "Bastard Daughters and the Possession of History in *Corregidora* and *Paradise*." *Signs: Journal of Women in Culture and Society* 28.1 (2002): 221-47. Print.

Zavarzadeh, Mas'ud, and Donald Morton. *Theory, (Post)Modernity, Opposition: An "Other" Introduction to Literary and Cultural Theory*. Washington, D.C.: Maisonneuve, 1991. Print.

❋ INDEX

Acker, Kathy, 3, 7, 143
  "A Few Notes on Two of My Books",
    118
  "Apparatus and Memory", 9, 107, 111,
    114, 117, 122, 123
  Blood and Guts in High School, 8, 11,
    18, 106–35, 139, 143
  Empire of the Senseless, 11, 18, 106–
    10, 117–35, 139, 143
Allen, Paula Gunn, 4, 15, 106, 126
  Off the Reservation, 103
  Song of the Turtle, 81
  The Woman Who Owned the Shadows,
    3, 9, 11, 17, 18, 79–82, 92–105,
    109, 133, 135, 142
Anzaldúa, Gloria, 5
  Borderlands, La Frontera, 1, 82, 104
  Making Face, Making Soul, Haciendo
    Caras, 10
Aristotle, 14, 138

Baldwin, James, 57
Bell, Bernard W., 140
Beloved. See Morrison, Toni
Berila, Beth, 140
Blood and Guts in High School. See
  Acker, Kathy
Bomberger, Ann, 7
Bordo, Susan, 133
Boutry, Katherine, 53, 77, 141, 142
Braidotti, Rosi, 2, 3, 5, 37, 42, 45, 111,
  140
Brande, David, 143
Brennan, Karen, 111, 143
Burrows, Victoria, 13
Butler, Judith, 5
  Gender Trouble, 11, 82
  Undoing Gender, 84
Butler, Octavia, 141

Caruth, Cathy, 141
Cha, Theresa Hak Kyung, 15, 109, 126,
  140
  Dictée, 2, 4, 8, 11, 16, 17, 22, 23, 33–
    46, 83, 87, 98, 102, 107, 108, 131,
    133–36, 139

Chang, Shu-li, 138
Cixous, Hélène, 3, 5, 10, 12, 22, 32, 34,
  41, 43, 46, 79
Clabough, Casey, 141
Collins, Patricia Hill
  "Meaning of Motherhood", 32
  "Shifting the Center", 47
Cook, Barbara, 142
Cooley, Nicole, 120, 143
Corregidora. See Jones, Gayl
Cosslett, Tess, 48

Daly, Mary, 109
Davis, Amanda J., 141
Davis, Angela Y., 52
Deleuze, Gilles, and Félix Guattari, 5, 108
Demetrakopoulos, Stephanie A., 138
Derrida, Jacques, 15, 130
Descartes, René, 14, 15, 117, 138
Di Prete, Laura, 10, 12
Dick, Leslie, 107
Dictée. See Cha, Theresa Hak Kyung
D'Lugo, Carol Clark, 8–9
Dubey, Madhu, 19, 53, 141, 142
Duvall, John N., 143

Empire of the Senseless. See Acker, Kathy
ethnicity, 4, 127
Everingham, Christine, 13

Fahy, Thomas, 53, 141
Federici, Silvia, 137
Felski, Rita, 137
feminism, 3, 4, 7, 15, 135, 137
Floyd, Kevin, 143
fragmented novel, 8–9
Franco, Dean, 127–28
Frankenstein, 1, 21, 135
Fraser, Nancy, 8
Frost, Elisabeth A., 42, 139, 140
Fultz, Lucille P., 30, 138

García, Cristina, 20
Gates, Jr., Henry Louis, 24
Goldberg, Elizabeth Swanson, 141
Gregson, Ian, 8, 137

Griffiths, Jennifer, 141
Grosz, Elizabeth, 3, 5, 14, 20, 130, 138
Guattari, Félix. *See* Deleuze, Gilles, and
    Félix Guattari
Gulf Dreams. *See* Pérez, Emma

Haraway, Donna, 8
Harris, Janice, 53, 75, 141, 142
Harris, Trudier, 51
Harryman, Carla, 143
Hawkins, Susan E., 143
Henderson, Carol E., 10, 31, 49, 50, 55,
    123, 138
Hernández, Ellie, 142
Hochberg, Gil Zehava, 141
Holford, Vanessa, 97, 103, 142
hooks, bell, 5
    Communion, 9, 11
    Feminist Theory, 3, 15, 20, 26, 51, 61,
        103
Hsiao-ching Li, Florence, 139
Hughes, Kathy, 143
Hulley, Kathleen, 143
Hurston, Zora Neale, 51, 61

Jameson, Fredric, 9, 137
    "Postmodernism and Consumer
        Society", 7
    Postmodernism, 6, 7
Jones, Gayl, 109, 124, 126
    "Gayl Jones Takes a Look", 51
    Corregidora, 3, 9, 10, 11, 17, 18, 19,
        21, 47–78, 83, 87, 93, 104, 107,
        118, 119, 133, 134, 135, 138, 141,
        142

Kennedy, Colleen, 143
Kim, Elaine H., and Norma Alarcón, 139
Kim, Sue J., 35, 140
Kocela, Christopher, 143

Lawson, Erica, 138
Lee, Kun Jong, 36, 38, 40, 139
Liscio, Lorraine, 138
Long, Lisa A., 53, 54, 55, 70, 141
Lowe, Lisa, 139
Lyotard, Jean-Francois, 6

Mathieson, Barbara Offutt, 138
matrilineal narrative, 48
McCaffery, Larry, 143
Merleau-Ponty, Maurice, 15, 38, 121
Milletti, Christina, 143

Mills, Fiona, and Keith Mitchell, 51
Minh-ha, Trinh, 5, 10, 21, 42
Morgenstern, Naomi, 28, 31, 53, 75, 77,
    78, 138, 139, 141, 142
Morrison, Toni, 8, 47, 109, 124, 126, 137
    "Unspeakable Things Unspoken", 1
    Beloved, 2, 11, 16, 17, 22–32, 45, 46,
        48, 50, 59, 67, 70, 72, 83, 87, 90,
        107, 133, 134, 135, 138, 139
Mukherjee, Srimati, 140
multiethnic, 2, 4, 6, 7, 9, 11, 19, 46, 80,
    106, 127, 134, 135
Mulvey, Laura, 35
Muñoz Cabrera, Patricia, 141

neo-slave narrative, 47, 140
Nicholson, Linda J., 8

Oh, Stella, 33, 140
othermother, 32

Park, Josephine Nock-Hee, 140
Pérez, Emma, 15, 106, 126
    Gulf Dreams, 2, 3, 4, 9, 11, 17, 18,
        79–105, 109, 133, 135, 138, 139,
        142
Perry, Phyllis Alesia, 15, 109, 124, 126
    Stigmata, 3, 9, 11, 17, 18, 47–78, 83,
        87, 97, 104, 107, 118, 133, 134,
        135, 138, 141
Phillips, Rod, 107
Phu, Thy, 140
Plato, 14, 138
Prince-Hughes, Tara, 96, 142
Pryse, Marjorie, 48
Punday, Daniel, 130

Redding, Arthur F., 122, 143
Rich, Adrienne, 12
Rottenberg, Catherine, 96
Rushdy, Ashraf H. A.
    "Daughters Signifyin(g) History", 24,
        32, 138, 139
    "Relate Sexual to Historical", 10, 141

Scarry, Elaine, 11, 137
Shelley, Mary Wollstonecraft, 1, 135
Sievers, Stefanie, 54, 141
Simon, Bruce, 141
Slattery, Dennis Patrick, 22, 27, 29, 31,
    138
Smith, Barbara, 80
Spahr, Juliana, 140

Stigmata. See Perry, Phyllis Alesia
Stratton, Jon, 128, 143
Streeter, Caroline, 141
Swaner, Scott, 40, 139, 140

Tan, Amy, 12, 137
Torres, Lourdes, 142
trauma, 10, 12, 48, 141
trauma theory, 141

Vickroy, Laurie, 8, 24, 37, 60, 134

Walker, Alice, 51, 142
    In Search of Our Mothers' Gardens, 1,
    22

womanism, 22
Wall, Cheryl, 75, 141
Watten, Barrett, 112
Wollen, Peter, 107, 143
Woman Who Owned the Shadows, The.
    See Allen, Paula Gunn
Worthington, Marjorie, 130, 143

Yu, Yi-Lin, 31
Yukins, Elizabeth, 48, 141

Zavarzadeh, Mas'ud, and Donald Morton,
    20, 40, 46

MODERN
AMERICAN
LITERATURE
New Approaches

Yoshinobu Hakutani, *General Editor*

The books in this series deal with many of the major writers known as American realists, modernists, and post-modernists from 1880 to the present. This category of writers will also include less known ethnic and minority writers, a majority of whom are African American, some are Native American, Mexican American, Japanese American, Chinese American, and others. The series might also include studies on well-known contemporary writers, such as James Dickey, Allen Ginsberg, Gary Snyder, John Barth, John Updike, and Joyce Carol Oates. In general, the series will reflect new critical approaches such as deconstructionism, new historicism, psychoanalytical criticism, gender criticism/feminism, and cultural criticism.

For additional information about this series or for the submission of manuscripts, please contact:

Peter Lang Publishing
P.O. Box 1246
Bel Air, MD 21014-1246

To order other books in this series, please contact our Customer Service Department at:

800-770-LANG (within the U.S.)
(212) 647-7706 (outside the U.S.)
(212) 647-7707 FAX

Or browse online by series at:

www.peterlang.com